notes on making movies

STRUCTURING TIME

notes on making movies

Michael Betancourt

Wildside Press

Published by:

Wildside Press

P.O. Box 301

Holicong PA 18928-0301

www.wildsidepress.com

FIRST EDITION

STRUCTURING TIME: notes on making movies   ISBN 0-8095-1117-7

CONTENTS

Introduction 9

THEORY

'Experimental' 13
Axiomatic Premises 14
Design 17
Light 18
Camera 20
Image 22
Sound 21
Sound/Image Relationships 25
Sound-Image Transformation 26
Frame 27
Frame Change Rate 28
Shape of the Image 31
Visual Space 32
3D 33
The Base Itself 34
Digital Processes 38
Cyberia 39
Pixel 42
Animation 44
Motion 45
Interlacing as a Source of Motion 47
Feedback Loops 49
Compression 51
Fractals 52
Recursive Development 54

Image-Temporal Matrix 55
Temporal Structures 57
Temporal Form 60
Modularity 62
Editing 63
Kuleshov Effect 64
Eisenstein's Montage 66
Jump Cuts 67
Graphic Match 68
Interlacing 69
Projection 70
Projector-Screen Relationships 72
Screen 73
Shaped Screens 75
Strobe-Based Movies 76
Self-Reference 78
Intentions 79
Subjectivity 82
Fascination 83
The Entertainer 84

PRACTICE

a note 87
The Story of It 89
A Self-Referential Film in 30 Sentences 91
Things 95
Post Film 97
Action Movie 98
Portrait Film 99
Postcard Film 100
Unseen Film Substitution 101
Victims 102
Illumination 103
New Movies 105
She, my memory 107
Happy People 108
Pr0n 109

Year 111
Telemetry 114
Selected Filmography 116

APPENDIX

a note 119
The _____ Manifesto 121
Statement 122
Media Mythos 124
Technology/Sex 126
Four-Letter Words 127
Strobe-Effect Movies 128
Wound Culture 129
Scripts for Year 130
Stan Brakhage Visionary Title Generator 134

acknowledgments 136

INTRODUCTION

Art Experiments

(1)

Most of these notes have a direct connection to my movies. They are the experimental premises and theory that guide the formal aspects of my work.

These notes are a general approach to motion pictures, one whose basis does not lie itself in mimetic realism. Because these theories attempt to be general, applicable to all sorts of movies, (not just my own), they include a lot of very basic ideas and observations that are meant to function axiomatically. They are empirically tied to my experiments with movies and statics.

(2)

Most of these notes create options (the parameters) without necessarily having to choose between them. What they present is a range of potentials.

A flexible framework reveals missed possibilities, and suggests avenues for development instead of being an obstacle to be overcome:

> The idea is that without specific and immediately clear potentials, the tendency would be to simply and unconsciously repeat the same movie rather than finding ways to make different movies every time.

Repetition via formula is boring for both the audience and the artist, and makes for unchallenging work.

(3)

Because these notes are a work in progress, constantly being rethought and reworked, setting them into a book has been very difficult.

Since notes are informal records of process/ideas, instead of academic arguments, the texts which follow take a variety of forms, often simply being lists or diagrams. They may be opaque in places. I have attempted to avoid this problem, I must admit that it is inevitable: these notes assume a familiarity with both the process of making movies and the history of avant-garde film and video within the context and theory of contemporary art.

THEORY

'EXPERIMENTAL'

There is a joke common to all American film schools that says "when you screw it all up, just call it 'experimental'," and there is a more than a little truth to this: all too often the idea of 'experimental' gets used to hide inability or mistakes. The problem with this use is simple: experiments are the only way to find new possibilities, but often experiments produce unexpected or negative results, especially in art.

My art is experimental: it acts as a testing ground for theoretical propositions about the nature and meaning of media, art, culture and is a continuous process of searching for new ways to do. This experimental nature means there is a strongly formal component to my aesthetic, even though formally-engaged art is out-of-fashion. However, a formal component does not mean that the work is nothing more than a mechanical process of investigating what can be done with movies; quite the contrary. The experimental character is directly connected to the meaning, because the form and content are linked at the level of praxis.

But because this formal aspect does exist, and is so crucial to the meaning and interpretative horizons of the art, a thorough investigation of formal potentials is the only method for reaching any kind of connection between form and meaning that does not simply assume the parameters of the media as such. Thus, the 'experimental' character is experimental in a scientific, empirical way: it is a test for the theoretical propositions as much as it guides those propositions.

"Art experiments" becomes a literal experiment with the form, meaning and nature of art, within the somewhat limited space of visual form.

AXIOMATIC PREMISES

Distinctions between different media have historically been based on the materials employed; however, this separation begins to break down when we encounter photography or film, and its difficulty is compounded with the myriad forms and uses the digital computer offers us. But if we speak of .mpeg, .avi, quick time, flash or shockwave files as separate media in the same way that watercolor, oil paint or bronze are different media, there is a sense that something vital is missing from this description—not least the fact that the work presented in one format can be fluidly translated into another. As contemporary film and video merge with digital technology, they escape the historical problems of film and video where there are definite, observable differences between the master and its copies. Digital "copies" are identical, perfect replications in every way (baring some kind of technological glitch). In the digital realm all copies are also the master.

If we take the development of digitality as both a "tool kit" and display technology—even for those works that also find their way into more traditional formats such as videocassettes or film—the indirectly physical nature of this technology (it presents itself as a mechanical interpretation of electrons stored in a physical medium) encourages a rethinking of medium-based distinctions. Once the tactile, physical object is discarded, we no longer have a material quality to distinguish one kind of image from another.

These notes constitute a Taxonomy of Motion based in a pragmatic phenomenology. The ways that our perceptions and interpretations are always already determined by our relationship to our history, culture, etc. are embedded in these notes and our perceptions—the "subjectivity" of a given artist working at a given moment is a crucial aspect of the working process. Instead of being a component to minimize, the subjective element is the crux that makes one artist's process different from another's—even if they begin from the same basis. A carefully description of the physical potentials of motion and its relationship to technology proposes ways to proceed with making movies. It is a matter of establishing initial conditions.

Where historical media were grouped based on their physical materials—watercolor, bronze, etc.—"new media" can be grouped around any set of observable physical characteristics: file format, size, etc.. Such a distinction is arbitrary (as much in historical media as in "new" ones); the division employed here is to separate

14

work based on its apparent movement.* This division creates two media: **movies** and **statics**.

'Real time' is the key to distinguishing between these forms. Many images move or change, but not in a fashion we can actually perceive. Thus: the movie is any image that appears to move, or is presented using an apparatus where such apparent movement is possible for us as humans to perceive. In contrast, the static is any image that does not appear to move, and/or is presented using an apparatus lacking the potential for movement, or which does not show such apparent movement; the opposite of a movie. The distinction between one and the other is obviously circular; it is a definition that follows from our innate ability to perceive motion. This set of relationships opens the question of physical supports in a new way that is independent of Modernist "purity" because it is possible (and easy) to imagine a movie that moves so slowly it appears to be a static, or a static that only moves when specific viewing conditions have been met.

Even though motion is paramount in this framework, the technological nature of movies and statics offers a set of points where the working process can intervene in the final form and the experience of the work. The following listing is not a hierarchy, but rather a sequential construction derived from conventional working processes:

CAMERA
IMAGE (BASE)
EDITING
PROJECTOR
SCREEN
SOUND

This list describes six formal aspects of all movies whose manipulation results in a finished work. While this is not the only possible formal listing, it is one that does not give priority to any specific aspect of the movie, nor does it privilege a particular technology as being necessarily better than another: these six aspects, their presence, combination or lack (the necessity for all six is questionable), is sufficient to describe anything that can be done which we might call a "movie" in the common usage of the word.

The history of film and video is, in part, a history of different artists claiming priority for a specific aspect of what is formally possible, then defining the use of that in a singular, specific way to the exclusion of all else as being the guarantee of the movie's being

* Betancourt, Michael. "Motion Perception in Movies and Painting: Towards a New Kinetic Art," in CTheory, October 21, 2002.

art. Montage, "long take" aesthetics, various sorts of realist cinema, or abstraction that negates the camera, or the real-time effects of closed-circuit TV have all been claimed as the necessary formal qualities in this history. This listing is not being presented with that purpose in mind; it is being advanced as a framework for thinking about the procedures of making, without exclusionary constraints on what is made.

It is a framework that creates potentials that can then be used in the fabrication of a movie, or ignored in favor of other, alternative possibilities. It is not a formal theory in the sense employed by Modernist art criticism—the formal here is a lower case 'f' that is concerned only with describing the most complete range of things an artist can do, not a historically mandated destiny based in physical materials. That Formalism played itself out in the 1970s with a series of reductions of film to the physical running of black, white or clear leader through a projector: an intellectual form that tells us very little about what else can be done, might be done, or has been done. Thus, the small-f formalism.

These areas have historically undergone aesthetic and technical evolution since the invention of movies in the 1890s. Each point of this list can be defined through a history of applications by different artists; such a survey describes a distinct formalist history that is divorced from economic and political distinctions created by the different film "worlds" of underground, avant-garde, independent, commercial, etc. that typically bias discussions of movies as a specific medium.

DESIGN

The attempt to create an alternative practice needs to be more than just an act of negation: not _____. Instead, theory works to provide guidelines for what may be done, without necessarily limiting what should be done.

Movies that do not involve actors, sets, stories do not involve direction in the sense it is commonly used. For this reason I prefer the concept of "design," because my movies are a fabrication much closer to visual or graphic art than to theater.

This concept of design attempts to articulate and inspire communication of real, seemingly unimaginable complexes covered up by a critical structure of experience (and its history) that we assume whenever we watch any movie. Over coming this proposition is the first problem for anymedia art. Instead of deconstructing itself, the goal here is to reinterpret existing materials (and component technologies), and extend the potentials of motion pictures beyond the limited framework of chemical film, and the everyday assumptions of commercial entertainment. Thus, the question of design versus direction is not just a matter of names.

LIGHT

Our visual experiences of the world begin with our ability to see light. In the case of movies, they are entirely composed from light (or its absence).

We perceive three kinds of light:

real

projection
(looking directly at some light producing source)
reflection
(light bounced off a non-emitting source)

imaginary

noise
(light seen because of the physical properties of our eyes)

There is a tendency to ignore the role of imaginary light in optical effects and phenomena, but it is the imaginary light that can be very compelling. Think of Stan Brakhage's description of his hand-painted films as an expression of this non-visual light.

Imaginary light is light we think we see, but is only a product of the misfiring and nerve-echoes in the rods and cones of our eyes. The spots we see when a camera's flash burns our eyes is the most obvious example. Such light is a result of the physical nature of sight. The grain in film (for example) and the artifacts produced by slowing video feedback are analogues for this physical property of our eyes [see Stan Brakhages' Metaphors on Vision for example].

Real light can be modulated and controlled, imaginary light cannot; it can only be suggested through analogy using real light (the experience of imaginary light is the private affair of each individual).

However, there are certain experiences (flash
ghosts for example) which result in imaginary light
that can be predicted, suggesting that there may
be ways of modulating and including such experiences in the experience of real light. Such work,
however, will invariably be technologically dependent and so is of limited life-span.

Any aesthetic build around light will deal with real light, but
also must consider the interactions of imaginary light—even
though these interactions will shift with the presentation technology and the person viewing it.

CAMERA

The modern camera, whether digital or analog, static or movie, originates with the camera obscura—the dark room—where projected images of the outside world would appear on a screen using lenses. The assumptions about visual space that appear in perspectival painting are repeated by the camera because both technologies—perspective and cameras—are connected to these historical darkened rooms that resemble movie theaters.

The issue of camera is intimately connected to image, but is independent of image. The camera is a technology whose function is the creation of a specific type of image.

Different camera technologies create and suggest a flexibility to this conceptualization:

> **multiplane animation camera**
>
> **slitscan camera**
>
> **optical printer**
>
> **high-speed camera**
>
> **infrared video camera**
>
> **etc.**

Cameras typically function through the framework of realism, but can be modified to become abstracting machine (the slitscan camera is one example).

When they are used to make a movie, cameras serve to determine aspects of all elements in the final movie. Most importantly, they provide the most basic frame change rate in the form of the **internal** (unless changed via editing) frame change rate. The technical profile of a camera is important to consider in terms of how it will shape the entire result.

Specialized application often require the development of specific camera able to meet the demands of that application. Different film stocks (8, 16, 35, 70 mm) each require different cameras, as do different tape formats. Special uses often result in the invention of new kinds of camera.

SOUND

All image-sound combinations are sync when they happen at the same moment. The issue is whether they're exactly, repeatably set, or are variables that change with every performance or screening of the movie.

Relative sync shifts with each performances, and is not physically connected to the image: for example, live performances where sound can be an accompaniment, improvisational, unplanned, or random; thus changing with every showing.

Absolute sync is connected permanently; it does not shift with performance: it is more like 'lip sync' in its attachment. (Recorded and physically connected to the image) and so cannot change.

Movies always include both relationships. The relative will always be present, even if its presence is undesired and is not meant to be part of the movie. The person talking behind you in a movie theater is a good example of this relationship between sound and image.

Both **relative** and **absolute** sync can be incorporated into the final piece. The movement between sync sound and async sound can be considered in terms of its relation to "typical" narrative filmmaking. In experimental works this relationship tends to be more ambiguous.

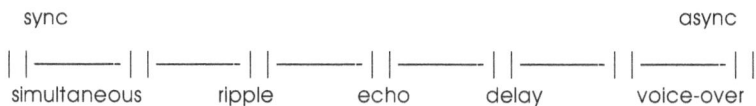

```
sync                                                              async

| |————- | |————- | |————- | |————- | |————- | |————- | |
  simultaneous      ripple      echo        delay       voice-over
```

The degree of difference in the relationship between the image and sound presents a range of possibilities with in the relationship of two tracks. The integration of **relative** and **absolute** sync can be described in these terms (sync to async) and within the same framework (for example the shifting relationships in Marguerite Duras' India Song).

IMAGE

The image exists as a result of a discrete physical layer that is always invisible: the base. This support is the medium where the image appears, and is dynamically connected to that image: any moment when the base becomes visible, it is as a result of its being transformed into image. Thus considerations of the image are also considerations of the base.

Images can be produced in two ways:

with a camera
without a camera

This pair of image-making methods applies equally well to any kind of imaging, whether digital video or analog video or film. The camera often appears in the process of making movies as an inevitable, and necessary, construct. It is not necessarily so; however, even when the camera is "absent" physically, many of digital processes either directly simulate a camera (as with the ray tracing of CGI simulations), or simulate the effects visible if a camera were to be used (as with many filters available in editing and effects programs).

The kinds of image can be converted from one to the other:

without —> with   (via rephotography or digitizing)

with   —> without   (via scratching, drawing, etc)

Movement between these potentials allows for hybrid works that incorporate aspects of both varieties of image making.

Movies made without a camera are either produced by hand (as in hand-drawn or painted film), or rendered digitally within the computer via CGI or processing.

Movies made with a camera involve light and some variety of photo-sensitive material: the film stock, CCD chip etc. The results of the encounter between light and sensor become the images.

A virtual encounter between a simulated camera

and virtual light acts to mimic the properties of a
real encounter, whatever the parameters of the virtual camera may be; however, because this encounter is virtual, it offers the possibility for cameras
whose form and function are impossible in the physical world; the dynamics of encounter between virtual sensor and virtual light can also be modified in
ways inconsistent with physical reality, and can
even violate the laws of physical reality if the
programmer chooses.

The digital variants of this paring become apparent through CGI.
Digital imaging either simulated the optical effects of cameras, or
it alters the image graphically as a two dimensional construct.

representational

abstract

The so-called "abstract" image is a useful fiction,
and even though it is often equated to non-representational imagery, it can (often does) have a representational character: it carries representational
meanings as a symbol for those things which defy or
lack conventional representational visualizing.

non-representation can only happen in the spaces where we do
not have the specific form of a movie to watch. For example:

Unseen Film Substitution
Abecedarium: U

This film instructs the audience to "substitute the memory of
a film they saw and enjoyed for this portion of the program." The
Unseen Film Substitution is necessarily **non-representational** in itself,
since any viewer following the instructions would not remember
having followed them (a paradox).

All movies communicate their content through representational means. It is the character of the image (**realist** or **abstract**) that varies from movie to movie.

Realist images do not necessarily require cameras.

Abstract images do not force a rejection of the camera.

A viewer deciding a movie is **Realist** or **Abstract** is a result of that viewer recognizing the depiction as related to their experience of the world (**realist**) or external to that experience (**abstract**). It is possible to have **abstract**-appearing movies that are actually **realist** (Telemetry is an example).

SOUND / IMAGE RELATIONSHIPS

All movies present two options when confronting the sound/image "problem." Not simply a matter of synchronous or asynchronous sound, there is also the question of their presence (or absence):

SOUND / NO SOUND   **IMAGE / NO IMAGE**

The pairing of sound and image present us with a series of potential relationships between the sounds intended to accompany a movie and its imagery. There are 4 possible versions of these potentials:

sound-image   "typical" movie

no sound-image   "silent" movie

no image-no sound   "conceptual" movie

no image-sound   "radio" (Walther Ruttman's Wochende)

Walther Ruttman's 1932 film Wochende is a sound work meant for projection to an audience in a movie theater; the film has no images to accompany the soundtrack, making it an example of a movie with sound, but no image.

The issue with audio/visual relationships is:

Does it play a significant role in the interpretation of the work, or is any relationship that appears a momentary, non-repeating phenomenon?

A relationship which only appears once (unless it is a one-time only artwork) is not typically significant to the work: i.e. a conversation held in front of an artwork is not usually a part of that work, and would be excluded from the interpretation in most circumstances.

SOUND-IMAGE
TRANSFORMATION

Technology offers not only the ability to synchronize sound and image with extreme precision, it also presents the ability to transform sound into image, image into sound, and information into either one. This exchange is possible because the electrical signals and data streams that are the material of electronic media can be "run through" decoders of any kind, often with anomalous results.

Any kind of data, most especially wave forms, can readily become sound because all that is required for this change is a shifting of values so one kind of wave (light, for example) can become another kind: sound.

Visual Music is a particular genre of movie that attempts to create visual art comparable to music. These works often adopt a parallel to music, either in the form of an aesthetic system, or more directly, through the construction of software/hardware that can be played like musical instruments.

FRAME

The smallest, most basic unit of movies is always the composite called the "frame"; even though these frames are always composed of smaller discrete units—either grain or pixels—these smaller units are always worked with as part of the totality is the image.

Frames are also the boundary between the image and the space that contains it. We conventionally recognize the presence the frame when an image either changes the shape of the frame or presents us with a series of smaller frames within the frame itself.

Framing Devices

masking

division into panels   (diptych, triptych, etc.)

division into smaller frames   ("windowing")

multiple projection

shaped projection

The frame is a constant for all kinds of imagery, whether movie or static. Consequently, some of the issues that can apply to movies also apply to statics. It is possible to adapt techniques and approaches from one form and apply them in the other.

Multiple projection and shaped screens are variations on the same concept: making changes to the frame by making a change to the projector, or by using several projectors whose images are combined to create a continuous image, or through altering the form of the screen where we see the image.

FRAME CHANGE RATE

The speed at which an image changes conditions our experience of it as a temporal object: we can only perceive changes happening in real time. Time lapse and speed ramping condense or expand the original time into a sped-up version where gradual changes become visible to us in real time.

In screenings with a frame change rate of 1 frame per day would be invisible to us as movement until projected at some faster rate (above 18 fps for smooth motion). We can only see motion when the frame change rate is below our visible threshold—approximately 12 fps.

Frame change rates which are equivalent to real time (or slower) we cannot perceive expect as real time. This is why narrative film can compress real time without causing the audience to be confused: movies already are a compression of real time. The physical event and the event of watching exist independently of one another. The samples which produce the motion are inherently variable.

All frame change rates are related to real time experience, so they can be seen in real time—yet they are abstractions of that real time experience, and so are understood by the audience in those terms—as artificial time, separate yet related to real time.

Rates of Change

frames per **second**
frames per **minute**
frames per **hour**
frames per **day**   the speed at which paintings, trees, etc.
frames per **week**   change is measured at a rate much
frames per **month**   slower than what we see in real time
frames per **year**   (i.e. we cannot see it change by sitting and
frames per **decade**   watching except in unusual circumstances)
frames per **century**
frames per . . .

The threshold point that the frame change rate represents has to do with the physical properties of our nervous-cogitative system. Our ability to see motion has evolved to perceive the world at a specific rate, the zero point we can call 'real time.'

> **Real Time** means that the motions we see in a movie correspond to the motions we would see if we were looking at the movie's subject directly and the motion were immanent rather than apparent.

Movies appear to move because their change-rate is faster than real time, while statics change at a speed much slower than real time.

There are three points where the Frame Change Rate can be adjusted:

the camera

the editing

the projection

The frame change rate is the speed at which images are displayed on screen. Under most circumstances, frame change rate remains constant. However, the motion apparent in the movie is not entirely determined by the projection speed. It is a result of the relationship between the projection speed, the camera speed and the movie's **internal** frame change rate.

The camera can be set to run at a specific speed (the camera's frame change rate); the images can be repeated, removed, of left unchanged in the editing (**speed ramping**); the projector can be adjusted to run at a specific speed (the projector's frame change rate). Both the camera and the projector do not alter the number of frames available in the movie, only the speed at which those frames are exposed/projected; only editing can change the actual frame change rate **internal** to the movie itself.

> The **internal** frame change rate is the physical relationship between successive images of the movie itself. This baseline is often determined by the camera, but can be altered during the course of production.

Speed ramping is the name for changing the **internal** frame change rate (speed) of a movie (either by increasing the number of frames in a sequence or reducing them). Unless a movie uses some form of **speed ramping** to change the **internal** frame change rate, the frame change rate of the editing remains the same as the frame change rate of the camera.

> A movie where every image is repeated for 90 frames without any change, and then projected at 30 fps, would present a static image for 3 seconds, followed by another, and so on, giving the movie a frame change rate of 1 frame per 3 seconds. These movies would appear as a succession of static images.

> 90 frames / 30 frames per second = 3 seconds per frame
> internal rate /   projection rate   = frame change rate

Under normal circumstances, these three rates are identical, and the motion appears on screen in a naturalistic, transparent fashion: we as audience do not become aware of the frame change rates, or even that they are subject to variation.

Frame change rate is crucial to the appearance of motion and how that motion appears to a viewer.

SHAPE OF THE IMAGE

The shape of the image is the form imposed on it by the frame itself.

orientation

horizontal (landscape)   most common projector orientation

vertical (portrait)

The orientation of the image can be adjusted within the image itself, or by reorienting the projector to present the image at a different angle than a horizontal plane. However, the image can also be reoriented within the frame itself.

aspect ratio

4:3   (TV)

16:9 (wide-screen, also HDTV)

2.35:1 (anamorphic)

These are the technical variables build-in to most equipment. Images can change these at the level of the image itself (via masking), thus allowing the presentation of a non-standard movie using standard equipment.

Multiple projectors can be combined to create a single image whose shape is irregular. It is also possible to change the aperture in the projector so the shape of the image itself is irregular.

Images change shape via masking, or by alternating their aspect ratio

Projectors change them by altering the projector itself

Screens change them physically. Shaped screens are a common feature of installation and performance work with movies.

VISUAL SPACE

Most cameras (and consequently most movies) are monocular: they present a single image for both the right and left eyes, creating the effect of visual space through graphic and representational means instead of sterioviews or "3D."

Space Appears

via perspective
via color recession
via scale   (larger vs. smaller)
via differential motion   (slower = more distant)
via on-screen placement (top = more distant)

Visible space is a conventionally-determined part of the image that also makes use of some features of how we cognitive interpret what we see.

Certain kinds of shape imply perspective, but aren't necessarily perspectival (i.e. Parallelograms), as do certain kinds of graphic relationship.

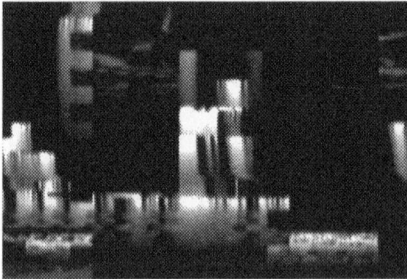

Year, stills from September demonstarting space and form based on purely graphic means.

3D

   3D movies can be made either with a special dual camera set-up for shooting two different images which are then seen with a headset that is sync to the projector, allowing the control of which image is seen by which eye (or with paired screens that have the same effect). Or, it can be made by working with color separation in animated films.

   Some technologies that produce 3D effects:

   Chromadepth™
   red-blue separation
   polarized images
   etc.

Each of these technologies creates images that are 3D in a different way, depending on how each one separate the way the viewer's eyes see the image. 3D depends on the left and right eyes seeing different versions of the same image.

   Of the three, Chromadepth™ is the most interesting since it allows a perception of space based on the RGB color separation of light. Because video equipment produced its images in color through mixing RGB pixels, when used with Chromadepth™ glasses, the 3D effects that appear are distinct from what happens with other technologies, or even with Chromadepth™ when used with traditional reflective media. (Year uses Chromadepth™ to create two variations of the same movie, one 2D and the other 3D.)

THE BASE ITSELF

The base is either a physical material such as the combination of emulsion and celluloid that are "film stock," or it is the combination of electronic signals and their meaning to the machines that decode them as with all forms of electronic imagery. The base is never a virtual construction since it necessarily has some properties that are connected (however indirectly) to physical reality.

Digital works present the image indirectly through a technological base that contains the image as a data stream. Thus the base for these works is digital--contained within the machineries that transform and/or store the data stream.

The digital file, like the data stream it represents and stores, is a physical object subject to various forms of loss and decay. When this happens we encounter the **glitch.**

Glitches are the digital equivalent of the physical scratches, cracks, aging, etc. that happen to any physical media like film.

Yet, the physical support for the images always remains invisible under optimal "normal" conditions. The appearance of grain, scratches, dust, marks, etc on film are regarded, from the point of view of "good" images, as being noise—things to minimize or avoid in the creation and exhibition of movies. This desire for conventionally defined clarity of image is common to all varieties of movie, and allows us to observe that the base, like all painterly techniques in realist painting, is ideally held to be transparent under standard, commercially-designated norms. And, further, that the appearance of the base will generally be treated as undesirable.

The acceptance and use of these characteristics normally left unseen is a common feature of what has variously been called avant-garde, experimental, underground, etc., an aesthetic choice at least partially made out of necessity (the expense of making movies was high), technical ineptitude (lack of training at using the equipment in standard commercial ways), or conscious desire to reject the commercial standard and affirm the material

nature of movies as such. The recognition that all three of these potential reasons for demonstrating the base of film does not invali-
date that choice or lessen the significance of the decision to
"leave in" the "errors." It is a decision that has had a dramatic impact on what is conventionally regarded as "authentic" and what
is not.

We can only encounter the base when it begins to impact
on what we encounter as image: the appearance of "base" is directly related to the ways that the images supported by that base
are destroyed, distorted or damaged by changes to the base, a
process that results in a radically different sort of image. This is a
technical issue that only becomes meaningful when it is considered from within the larger framework of a specific work: the particular uses of "base" in a specific movie, by a particular artist.

Revelation of Artifice

The Modernist conception of self-reference: that the artwork makes explicit reference to its own construction and internal
relationships is only partially a matter of formalist purity and reduc-
tion (although it can support such approaches). The self-referential
is a means to invent meanings from an interaction between an image and its base (an observation that applies equally well to painting or photography). By making the audience aware of the
manufacture and method for a specific movie as image allows the
intrusion of what the base means in conventional works without
having to adopt an aesthetic system that would require the
removal of the "noise."

Feedback, a characteristic potential of all recording systems, will only reveal the base under certain, very limited conditions. The most common forms of feedback involve taking a live
camera (or microphone) and applying the output signal to the input , typically by pointing it at a video screen (or speaker). The im-
ages/noises produced by feedback are not a function of the
base; they are magnifications of faults and details contained inside the display mechanism—the cathode ray tube, speaker, projector—rather than necessarily aspects of the base. Only under
through the limited condition of a re-recording and looping an already existing image series—whether film or video—will the feedback begin to demonstrate the base. This happens because the
work being "looped" is not a live signal but a recorded one. Imper-
fections in specific frames of the movie will then magnify in the
same ways that a live feedback look magnifies details of the display. In the case of DV, depending on the compression of the signal, this feedback may quickly begin to exhibit details produced
by how the images are stored.

The nature of the base lies in its unwillingness to be easily manipulated. While it is possible to simulate the appearance of the base for film with digital systems, the actual base of DV remains unseen in these works. What the digital system does by imitation is to make the physical appearances of base in film become nothing more or less than a specific stylistic effect of DV. While this does allow an ease of use and offer new potentials for these base effects, on another level, it fosters a misrecognition of what the base is and its relationship to the images it supports, encouraging a closing off of the specific explorations of movies that artists working with the potentials of the image-base dynamic represent.

Film

Those formal aspects of the film material that are linked to some aspects of its base (or the process of assembling a movie)—frame lines, tape splices, dirt, fingerprints etc.—have been claimed by some filmmakers as the only way to make film "pure." Often these arguments for purity proceed from the basic idea that the material of film, the base which supports the emulsion, is the most fundamental aspect of what film is, and its manipulation is a way to avoid the contamination of other media (such as video). This view elevates the intrusion of the base into the visible to the standard of being "art."

However, these arguments are based on the idea that the projection is separate from the film, separable from the film. But when we consider what it is that makes our experience of film different from sculpture or painting, we realize that this experience is based around the projection of a film and its development within the duration of that projection.

This is not to say that the material aspects of the filmstrip are not an inherent part of the experience of seeing a film. Quite the opposite. Simply that by placing the material aspects of the film above the way that a film develops within a specific duration. Films whose development is based entirely on the material—as we watch the film it gradually accumulated more and more dirt within the film field, for example—do show us how a film ages as it is projected, and encourages us to think about the material aspects of film, but they tell us very little about the nature of the film experience; their focus is the material of the film rather than the experience of the material.

The physicality of the material is not the film, although it does have a very clear relationship to it. This 1:1 relationship between the material of the filmstrip and the film has led some to consider that the filmstrip is equivalent to the film itself because—what could be more obvious—any mark made on the filmstrip appears within the film.

However, when we consider the filmstrip as such we immediately realize that it is not the film. It is transparent, not luminous. It is still, the film is in motion. It has a serial character to the images, while the film does not. The filmstrip is a template for the film, rather than the film itself; this is why any marks made to the strip will appear in the film, and their inclusion within a motion picture can connect to the development of the film itself.

When the material of the film intrudes into the projection it is generally recognized as "noise" since, under normal conditions it is "noise," given the most common experience of watching a film projected. However, there are situations where this material "noise" becomes an important part of the development of the film as a whole, and that is when the film is using these material signifiers of its projection to assert its status as a film; that is, for self-reference.

DV

When we speak about the "base" in movies, we have to consider first what kind of physical work we're discussing: film, video, DV, something else or hybrid between these. This consideration is essential to discussion about the base because the base of a movie is the physical support that contains the images, sounds, etc.; in the case of film it is the perforated material that contains the photographs projected on screen; for video it is the magnetic tape containing the electronic signal—a common feature uniting both analog and DV, however, for DV this "base" is complicated by the imposition of the compression that lies between the image and its recorded signal. Unlike analog video where manipulation of the magnetic tape can produce visible effects in the image, similar alterations to DV tape eliminates the image entirely: for all practical purposes, the base of DV is the compression codec.

DIGITAL PROCESSES

The digital computer offers the combined potentials of optical printer, paik raster, flatbed editor, and animation stand. These formerly distinct devices, when combined in this fashion, provide an unprecedented plastic ability in the handling of movies.

Computer movies can be manipulated at the level of individual pixels, and transformed using algorithms that mimic the effects of traditional media. To do so, however, fails to recognize the radical character of this process to loop into itself, and create effects that exceed these simulations.

By isolating specific tiny movements in the original source material it is possible to make technologically-derived movies where the image is a result of the digital processes of compression, de-compression, "optical printing," and sampling. The movies that result are directly a result of the technology employed (thus formally consistent and dependent) in the same ways that abstract photography can be consistent and dependent on the physical properties of chemical processing.

CYBERIA

There is a set of engineering issues that are common to all technological arts in the digital age: sampling, fragmentation and reassembly, data compression and expansion... and the glitch. We like the glitch, not because it formalistically reminds us what we are seeing is an artifact (it does), but because in our encounter and by developing our relationship to the glitch, we can enter into a dialogue with our technology on its own terms, negotiating for points of contact between what we-as-audience will accept and what we reject as technological failure, as an interruption to our fantasies of dominance, power, mastery.

The digital pretends to allow us access to abilities beyond our competence because it is so technically perfect. In searching out the glitch we find ourselves in cyberia, encountering the artifacts left-over from our technological abstraction. This experience has the potential to become a dominant paradigm for our encounters with mediated reality. When we encounter the glitch the limits of our technology become apparent to us. It causes a manifestation of the interpretative limits to our technology and our ability to prevent that technology from degrading over time. What we call a glitch is a variety of entropy revealing the secret language of digital technology.

Glitch

In its perfection, the digital introduced new kinds of signal-to-noise degradation. This decay was unexpected, a reminder of the connections between the virtual and the physical that digital media seeks to hide. By exploring these realms we can discover the limits of our technical competence; the points where our technology impedes us rather than enables functionality. While in principle digital "objects" are infinitely reproducible, the reality is these "objects" exist as real-word electrical signals subject to physical effects. One copy may be exactly the same as another, but only so long as nothing interferes with that copy to degrade it.

The glitch shows us the paradox beneath the claim of perfect replication, exact copying, infinite availability. While the digital does allow complete, perfect replication, it also offers possibilities for complete loss, total system crash. The glitch is the transient failing, the momentary lapse that allows us to see underneath the mask at the reality hidden inside the digital representation: How much data has been lost to faulty storage, poor transmission, or obsolete technology? How much more will we lose in the future? These are the questions of cyberia that make us

39

aware of the glitch. We find at the heart of the digital a paradox unresolved—the illusion of infinite reproducibility, perpetual reproduction and replication—forces us to confront the glitch as the inevitable limit to our extended reach.

Glitch is technology talking back to our fantasies of the infinite.

Once we discover the glitch, like addicts, we want more. For technojunkies, the glitch is endlessly fascinating, the final aspect of the real playing into the virtual realities we're told to desire. It is the latest Gnostic moment, for hatred of the physical body runs deep, a desire to place "mind and spirit" above the corporeal, ignoring the intimate connections all our virtualities have to mundane physicality. (Cyberspace was born a fantasy from its start in Neuromancer.) The glitch brings us back into reality from cyberia. The desert of virtuality grows only vacuum flowers, glowing and effervescent, side-effects of other processes. We only become aware of this link to the real when the glitch interrupts our fantasy with a 404 Error—blue screen of death—pixelization: the digital medium impinging on our transparent reveries before the screen. The glitch shows us the screen, not our fantasy displayed on it. Broadband, DSL, T-1 each only serve to mask the technological window into cyberia, bringing things faster, so we see less of the medium, and more media. We set the digital in motion and it generates itself on our command.

Rip, Mix, Burn

The extension of virtual media will eventually change the marketplace as we know it, leaving behind only fetish objects whose actual contents are infinitely available: the lessons of mp3 music swapping are already readily visible. It provides suggestions about what the future may be like when media such as music is free, (the songs available now, here... everywhere, legal or not), the only reason to purchase the album is to own an object, singular and special in itself as a thing independent of the music it might contain. Physical recordings begin to take on the same quaint quality we reserve for hand-blown glass, traditional carvings, paintings. Commercial CDs become specialty products, luxuries for enthusiasts, the same way that vinyl records are now a minority interest item, important only to specific subcultures (the DJ and scratch subcultures are the most obvious examples). The music and digital "content" are secondary to our purchase. In a triumph of form over content, we buy not for its contents, but for the package. Design culture triumphs. This paradigm is a potential (nacient) future for all digital media. In this future, the glitch plays a prominent role in our technological encounters.

Cyberia

When the glitch comes, we have fully entered into cyberia. It is a state without a direct physicality (in the way groves cut in vinyl are physical)—everything we encounter in digital media is a second-order (re)presentation given to us by ingenious devices that speak their own digital language inaccessible to humanity, but wholly dependent on us for its existence. This is a machine world built to service us even as we find new uses for it. It is one where the glitch reigns supreme, the final ruler of cyberia, because to destroy a thing is to control it. The glitch that arises from machine failure reminds us of our powerlessness before the technology we have built.

Neither celebration nor fear are appropriate responses to this development. It is the side-effect, the afterburn, of our technology reaching a kind of maturity. It gives us the potential to remake portions of our civilization in different terms, much the same way the printing press enabled a basic change in European civilization that has produced, ultimately, the digital. The movement towards abstraction is implicit in this development; the glitch is always an abstraction—it is the eruption of digital representations into the realm of human encounter: the ways the digital interprets its data enables our meeting in cyberia.

As artists we can choose to engage this glitch preemptively, before its dominance becomes immediately apparent. Art may provide a means to understand and frame our phenomenal relationship to the glitch in terms other than as-interruption in the seamless transparency of cyberia. We need encounters with the glitch that are independent of its hijacking of our experiences, a terrorist that destroys our encounter with digital media.

A formalist answer to this problem neglects the human angle. The glitch is a way to see what our technology typically hides from us: the actual functioning of its processes, events that come into motion only because we have set them into motion. Formalism makes machines that exclude the human, while these machines exist only to extend our human capabilities. We are already cyborgs whose cyberspace is a vast, unexplored, mechanized wasteland that stands apart from human experience. Cyberia is a place we can only see through the glitch.

As our civilization becomes increasingly a resident of cyberia we create new names for our experiences. "Art" should be one of those names. It offers us a way of reaching an understanding of our technology and our relationship to it.

PIXEL

While the antecedent for the pixels in our televisions, computers and digital cameras may appear to be the silver halide grains of photography, this is not entirely correct. The phosphor dots used in video monitors do originate with the same research that produced photography. However, this is not the same as originating with the "grain" of photography. Early photography is remarkably crisp: even when blurry or unfocused it is not what we would call "grainy." When the grain does appear in these early images, it is less a description of the image we see and more a haze that interferes with our ability to see the picture. Unlike pixels, the grain of early photography does not appear as the fundamental "bit" of the image; it is the work of Post-Impressionist painter Georges Seurat that advances the best historical model for the concept of the pixel as a luminous dot, which, when visually combined by the audience forms an image.

Understanding the origins of the concept for pixel requires an understanding of their approach to visual phenomena. It is specifically "atomic" in the nineteenth century pre-quantum conception of physical reality: that the whole world can be broken down into discrete units, called "atoms" that are self-contained, divisible from one another and individually knowable. The Periodic Table of the Elements, a major achievement of nineteenth century physical chemistry, is an artifact enshrining this approach. It is a way of dividing the world up into discrete physical units with unique characteristics, categorizing them based on individual properties. They can recombine into something new. The concept of pixels as the building blocks of images reflects this approach to the world.

Every pixel in a color image can be described as a set of three discrete numerical values whose separation is based on wavelength. The three primary colors of light—red, green and blue—optically mix as a result of our physical distance from the actual spots that are emitting the light. This effect creates not only apparently solid colors, but allows us to see images on screen. It is a result of optical convergence. The combination of colors creates hues and shadowing, allowing a high degree of realism. Because these points of color are distinct and separate from one another, they can be manipulated independently of one another to create composite effects impossible otherwise. This description of how pixels function is identical to Seurat's theoretical model for color that resulted in his so-called "pointillist" technique.

The Impressionist painter's insistent use of brush strokes to form imagery that disintegrates into individual marks on close examination becomes in Seurat's painting an emergent phenomenon of our encounter. on closer inspection, the apparent colors, shapes, and forms vanish, and we perceive separate spots of color—the basic elements of the image—as individuals. Our inability to see these individual dots of color is an inherent effect of the physical construction of our eyes. We do not have "enough resolution" in our eyes to see these dots qua dots at a distance. These images exploit our limitations to create their effects.

We view digital images. What we encounter are small spots of light that correspond to the component parts of a Seurat painting in both form and function. We do not typically perceive these pictures as a series of discrete values. In fact we generally regard those images where we see the structure of the image, its pixels, as a technological failure. The pixels appear as artifacts: even though the images our technology presents are composed from pixels we do not expect to see them. This fact is significant. It connects our encounter with pixels with the older tradition of realism that valued "transparent" techniques where the execution did not force us to become aware of it in fabricating the image. Seurat, like Signac, belongs to this realist tradition.

Pixels are a technological adaptation of the phenomena Seurat exploits. The images we encounter are products of two related approaches to imaging: raster and vector graphics. These two ways to describe visual imagery are in fundamental opposition, repeating the painting:photography dialectic in a new technology. Their differences clarify the connection between Seurat's painting and the pixel itself.

The optical mixture of these dots is Seurat's theoretical framework. The assembly of the components happens as the audience views the image. Relative scale and proximity plays a role in determining the fusion of these points of color. We see the images in Seurat for the same reason and based in the same physiological phenomenon that we can see them on any screen—whether a video monitor at home or a light panel in a sports stadium. Raster graphics generate images identically to Seurat: from collections of tiny points of color whose individuality can be manipulated separately, but we see them additively in combination.

ANIMATION

All movies are forms of animation

    Animation is a function of the frame change rate. The appearance of motion depends on the relationship between successive frames coupled with the frame change rate. Successive images present a series of possibilities. Note that as the differences between the succeeding images increases, what results is a shift from complete stasis, into limited motion, through normal motion and beyond, into pixelization where every image is totally different:

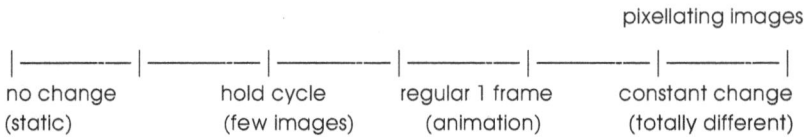

                                                                    pixellating images

```
|————|————|————|————|————|————|
no change        hold cycle      regular 1 frame      constant change
(static)         (few images)    (animation)          (totally different)
```

    There are several assumptions implicit in this diagram: the foundation of all movies is the rapid presentation of static imagery; images must be in a sequence based on change and similarity; motion appears because we mentally fit the images together.

    The apparent motion of a movie creates the illusion of an immanent encounter, but this is an illusion we do not normally experience as an illusion.

    Animation is always a result of the frame change rate being such that when viewed, the resulting images present an apparent motion we accept as identical to what we see with physically moving objects. In practical terms this means a frame change rate of approximately 12-18 frames per second.

    Standard motion picture film runs as 24 fps, and NTSC video runs at approximately 30 fps.

    The creation of movement relates to the ways that animation can contrast movement with stasis.

MOTION

Change between successive frames is the generator of motion.
(Without change, there can be no movement.)

This diagram is a variation of the diagram for animation:

Degree of Change

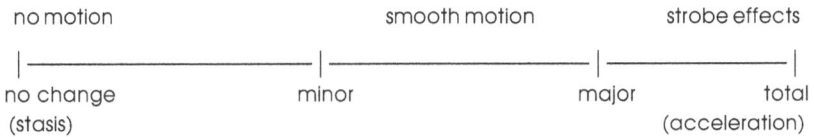

no motion		smooth motion		strobe effects
|———————————|		———————————|		———————|
no change (stasis)		minor		major		total (acceleration)

As the degree of change increases, the motion gradually becomes smoother and more fluid, but at the same time, the speed of apparent motion gradually increases until, where every frame is uniquely different from every other frame, the result is a strobing of imagery, but a lack of apparent motion. The appearance of motion results from variable degrees of change within a single image. Motion appears in relation to areas of stasis (or semi-stasis) within the frame.

Speed is equally variable, depending on contrast within the frame and across the duration of the image. This is a relative effect; slowing down a sequence can create the appearance of greater speed in those following without necessarily accelerating:

Slow down to go faster.

Is one way to explain this contextual part of our perceptions of motion, speed, and time.

Video (both analog and digital) offers potentials for developing movement based on the technology of video itself in a way impossible with media such as film.

Range of Potentials

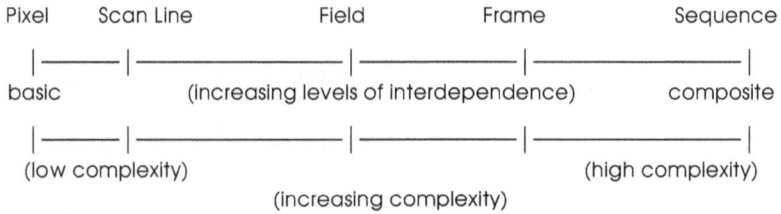

Pixel	Scan Line	Field	Frame	Sequence

|——|————————|——————|——————|—————|
basic   (increasing levels of interdependence)   composite

|——|————————|——————|——————|—————|
(low complexity)   (high complexity)
(increasing complexity)

The range described above scales from the simplest part of video to the most complex, but each point in this range is directly related to the those previous to it. Each stage depends on the lower, more basic points. It is possible to intervene in the creation and structure of video at any point in the scale, creating effects that extend to the more complex end of the scale.

The manipulation of the image at each stage of this range is a shift in complexity. The most basic element of video that can be altered is the individual pixel; the most commonly manipulated is the sequence of images (via editing). Each change to the individual image impacts the motion of the sequence as a whole. The movement we see in a movie is a result of individual changes taken together and viewed as a sequence.

INTERLACING AS A
SOURCE OF MOTION

Both PAL and NTSC video are composed of two paired fields which together form one frame of video: A and B.

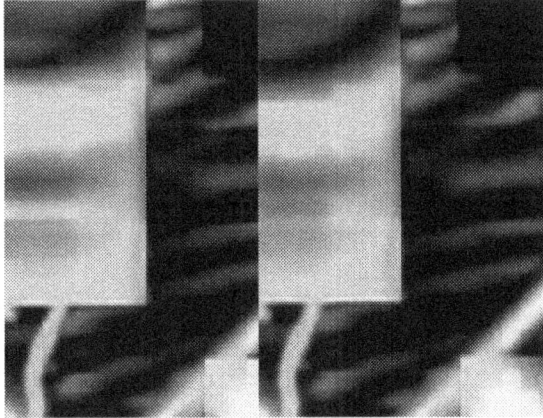

This is a side-by-side comparison of two fields from the same frame: A is on the left, B is on the right. Note the subtle differences between them.

The frames of interlaced video share an inherent, latent motion in the form of the scan-fields that are separated both in time (one then the other) and physically on screen (top and bottom).

Images displayed/recorded as interlaced can be separated and this latent motion expanded using a digital computer. Motion of this type oscillates between these two positions even when the image is stationary (static), but will complicate and mirror motion that already exists in the frame.

Some forms of digital processing (and analog) will handle these paired fields independently, and working with them can create unusual effects.

8-bit Atari video games handle the fields separately, and may even have different content in each field.

Speed ramping interlaced video at a rate below 50% of the original speed can cause these latent motions to become actual as each field will become an individual frame (unless the software recomputes all the fields).

The technical structure of the image (interlaced, not interlaced) can have dramatic effects on the resulting movie, and the flicker resulting from the computer digitally handling different fields in different ways may be a problem for some movies.

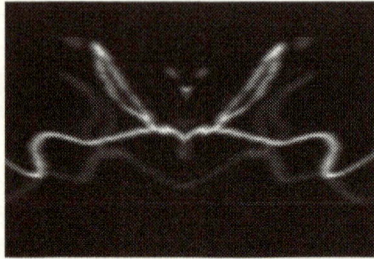

A deinterlaced frame from the final version of Forces of Symmetry.

Forces of Symmetry had to be manually deinterlaced frame by frame because the processing created a second, different, motion in each frame. Removing this second field was necessary to eliminate the different motion of the B field.

FEEDBACK LOOPS

Feedback loops are possible with any kind of recording technology; the difference between one technology and another (in this regard) is how easily these loops can be created and manipulated.

There are two kinds of feedback:

direct

indirect

Direct feedback appears automatically whenever a live camera (for example) is connected to its output by pointing it at a screen. A recursive image appears, and whatever happens to appear in the screen repeats towards infinity.

Indirect feedback must be consciously created by taking a processed, recording and then repeating the processing multiple times, creating similar effects to direct feedback, but with a much higher degree of control and guidance than is possible with direct feedback.

Different imaging equipment handles the issue of feedback differently, not simply in the distinction of analog vs. digital, but between different analog or digital machines. These differences come from the nature of feedback itself: it is a technological magnification of subtleties inherent in the particular signal-to-noise ratio of a specific machine or specific series of processes.

Feedback is a process that can force unseen aspects of the technology to become visible through its magnification of subtlety.

Indirect feedback (looping processes) creates controlled versions of what is uncontrollable in direct feedback. The distinction between the two is more than simply a matter of control; it is a matter of aesthetics.

Direct feedback is largely uncooperative when subjected to a rigorous and precise aesthetic manipulation.

The recompression of DV over successive generations can result in the appearance of features derived from the compression codec itself; while not generally considered feedback per se, these compression artifacts emerge and gain prominence for the same reasons as feedback, and so may be regarded as a form of **indirect feedback.**

COMPRESSION

Digital media come in two varieties: compressed and uncompressed.

Uncompressed files remain constant because at no point is their content being altered for storage.

Compressed files, however can change as a result of the data loss that is inherent to all methods of compression: in order to make the file being stored much smaller than it would otherwise be, compression algorithm use sets of rules called "codecs" to reduce the amount of information required to represent the media. This process requires that information be transcribed from one form into another, smaller one. This process inherently involves information loss and offers possibilities for errors to damage or change the media.

Compression-based effects that appear in a movie or static are generally called either "artifacts" or "glitches" because they emerge from the technology itself.

DV compression appears in the movie as a segmentation of tonal values, dividing the image into large blocks that are resistant to manipulation and repair because they are an inherent feature of the video codec that stores and presents the movie. It is possible to recognize in these blocks the underlying graphic structure of the image and its development.

Consequently, and processing that requires compression as an intermediary stage will have to either accept the uncontrollable additions made by the codec, or work without compression.

"Glitches"

These compression artifacts present us with a readymade image of interpretation and memory made visible by the technical properties of our technology. Digital signal decay is an almost inevitable consequence of working with compressed video, and their presence is magnified by successive generations of processing.

FRACTALS

Fractal geometries are self-contained models of infinity that are also programmatically systematic in the manner of serial art. At the same time, they have an irrational character in that they are truly infinite, but still a product of rational, limited processes. This formal dialectic between rationality and irrationality lies at the heart of all forms of abstraction when examined experientially since it is the character of the abstract to attempt to represent those things that are unrepresentable.

From the point of view of science and math, fractals are fascinating things, their relevance immediately obvious, but in art, this is not the case. Contemporary art, under the guidance of various Post-Modernisms, has a tendency to present science, math, and other empirical investigations as fantasy systems, apparently the result of various social forces or psychopathologies. This split between art and science is the recurring heritage of the Romantic movement in the nineteenth century, and its reemergence in contemporary art suggests that there has been a reversion to a premodernist position where art and science are two incompatible cultures. Within such a framework, fractals (in fact science as a whole) is irrelevant. The artist's (or the critic-theorist's) interpretations—however ill informed—are all that matter.

This then is one recognizable condition of the present, its recognition thus offers various alternative positions in relation to science: the artist-scientist (an artist who also actively engages in doing science, presents work at scientific conferences as part of the art, etc.); the more traditional artist-influenced-by-science (an artist who draws on and attempts to employ science as part of the art, not simply in its manufacture); and then there is the scientist-artist (a scientist who adapts the science into accessible forms of art and exhibits it as such). These three possibilities are not meant to be exhaustive, simply illustrative of potentials in the art-science relationship where the "two cultures" are not regarded as separate or antithetical.

Within such a framework, fractals occupy only a marginal position, their use thus far has been only as curiosities: brightly colored geometric patterns used to add visual excitement to club flyers, music packaging, etc. but not as a source for making art. The descriptive principles derived from these graphics can be applied to art, if they are used as production techniques.

Recursive Symmetry is the most obvious characteristic of fractal graphics: there is an overall pattern that repeats at different sizes throughout the image, a result of the whole being built from a limited number of specific components, which also repeat at different scales. It is this characteristic that gives the fractal is modular character, and is the common factor between fractals and other representations of infinity.

Complexity arises from different structures interacting within the same space. These create the apparent "randomness" that is at the same time orderly. The overlaying of recursive structures within a fractal maintains a consistent structure even though at any given point within that structure what we encounter may be completely unique. The visual complexity of fractals comes from our simultaneous recognition of the overall structures within the individual variations.

It is possible to create visual art using fractals as a reference point without necessarily using the fractals themselves. And in the case of movies, there are opportunities to create fractal effects both within the specific space of the individual image and across the structure of the movie as a whole.

RECURSIVE DEVELOPMENT

Recursion is a natural feature of fractals, but it is a potential in all motion images, especially in the compressed digital file that records changes between successive frames. All frames in a movie, taken in tot (atemporally) are a recursive representation of the entirety of the motion: it's development in visual space and across time.

The progenitor for this kind of representation in movies is Marey, rather than Muybridge, because in his photographs the image describes both the movement, its path in time and its development along that path.

Feedback loops are inherentlyrecursive; their effects are a product of the way recursion magnifies minor details and differences to the point that they become the dominant character of an image.

IMAGE-TEMPORAL MATRIX

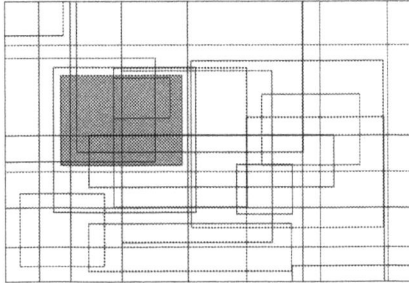

This diagram illustrates an image-temporal matrix
from Telemetry.
The grey area highlights one temporal lens.

This concept originates in Cubist painting's restructuring of space. The frame is broken into smaller pieces that function as **temporal lenses**.

This construction offers 2 possibilities:

(1) The repetition of the image from elsewhere in the frame-construction.

(2) Duration modification (faster/slower via speed ramping) and/or a temporal shift presenting moments drawn from other points in the evolution of the image.

These two potentials generate an x-y grid of potential transformations. The z-axis for this structure appears through the recursive potential of this construction.

Any type of image can be subjected to this structure; it is not exclusively a construction for abstract movies, although it is most easily applied to them.

The **temporal lenses** are fractally organized to produce images of recession and recursive symmetry (although other possibilities do also exist, this use results in a fully-articulated structure that can present all moments of temporal development at once).

Working with **temporal lenses** creates a grid-like matrix. This structure can then be looped via indirect feedback to create successive levels of structure. The full elaboration of an image-temporal matrix requires this looping to include changes to the duration, placement, etc of each lens (and/or its contents).

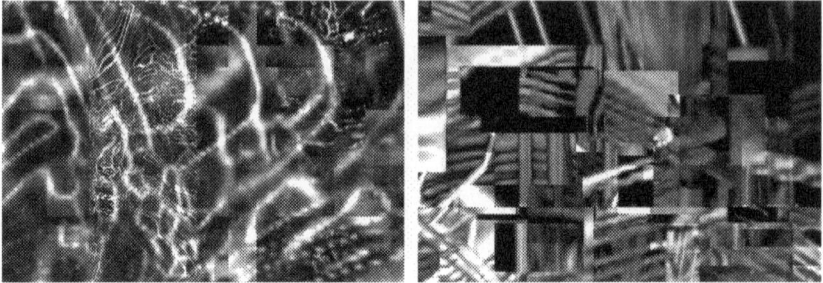

These frames are taken from Telemetry.
They allow a comparison of (3) and (4) respectively.

These changes then offer other potentials because each stage of the elaboration is available as source material for more development.

(3) The assertion of a dominant image serves to break the all-over construction, so the whole oscillates temporally between unification and segmentation

(4) The visibility of explicit segmentation serves to break traditional composition in favor of an all-over construction (as in the painting of Pollock)

The temporal element is crucial to these arrangements and is the difference between a Cubist structure, Pollock's drip paintings, and this form. It is a structure that can serve as a representation (suggestion) of infinity, but can easily become a steady-state structure where development through time is preempted by the presentation of that development all-at-once.

TEMPORAL STRUCTURES

All movies, because they are in motion, develop through time. However, within that parameter, we can make some distinctions between videos that present themselves all-at-once and those where their development is significant. This distinction enables us to differentiate some general temporal structures for movies based on how they engage with time:

Steady-State

> **temporal**
>
> **atemporal**

> **Atemporal** works are grasped in their entirely in an instant (as with a painting) even though they are in motion.

> **Temporal** works, while they do present their entirety in an instant, cannot be grasped in the same immediate way that a painting can be: the movement they present is significant to their form and meaning.

Steady-state movies present essentially one image that, while in motion, remains constrained to a limited number of potentials. Movies where the frame change rate is very low and the result appears essentially stationary and movies where there is no significant difference between one moment and another are equally examples of steady-state structures. These movies can be approached in the same way that painting or other static art can be.

Durational

linear

loop

> **Linear** works have specific beginnings, middles and ends, and require their audience to watch from the beginning through their entire duration.
>
> **Loops** involve duration and they do develop, but are also constrained to repeat cyclically so while they lack specific beginnings, middles and ends, they are not graspable as singular moments: loops involve temporal elaboration and development.

Durational works have a specific development that happens over the length of the movie. This kind of movie is the most familiar (if not necessarily the most common) since all entertainment, being narrative fiction, has a particular duration and follows a specific development in that time.

The difference between the Loop and the Temporal steady-state work is important: while the loop lacks beginning, middle and end, it does evolve through time. The Temporal steady-state works does not evolve-it simply presents a single state: a scrolling LED sign is a good example of a Temporal steady-state work. It is possible to understand it's form instantly, but time modifies that experience without altering its form.

Typically we move between both the **vertical** and **horizontal** poles of looking in relation to time, even within a single frame. Our shifts in recognition, understanding, seeing are a result of length of viewing time.

Vertical Time	**Horizontal Time**
immediate	duration
(image)	**(motion)**
Steady-State	Durational
Structures	Structures

Vertical Time   we understand instantly; immediate time is also a form of still time (i.e. time where duration is irrelevant)

Horizontal Time   we understand in relation to other images, or after a period of contemplation (i.e. duration is significant)

Images can be understood in either way: they encourage one or another interpretation as their initial reading/rendering with other readings following (this is only natural given that we look at different images in different ways depending on how they appear formally) such interpretations are reified by our typical experiences (everyday interpretation gives the appearance of being determinate) but, often we use both types of time in concert. With visual art these relationships shift more strongly.

TEMPORAL FORM

The spectrum of possibilities in the structural realm of the movie itself repeats the relationship suggested by the frame change rate. This requires a recognition that it is more than simply a "device" that provides motion.

Essential to the concept of the Frame Change Rate is the idea of alteration in time.

The concept of alteration through time also describes the structural arrangement of sequences, shots, etc. within the work as a whole. While there is an almost unlimited series of potential ways to create structures in time, depending on the duration of time between the changes, several structures begin to emerge.

These are all regular, modular repetitions selected from this range of possibilities. These forms can exist alone, or in combination creating complex rhythmic patterns.

"Punctuated Equilibrium Structure"

|—|—|—|—|—|—|—|—|—|—|—|—|—|—>

Evenly spaced changes where Change comes on an even interval. As the space between these intervals increases, the form shifts to become:

"Serial Structure"

| ——— | ——— | ——— | ——— >

Major changes within an otherwise similar progression lies in the interval between changes. As the intervals increase structure shifts to become serial. As these intervals become longer, or transform themselves to become indistinguishable from one another, the form shifts again.

It becomes a singular unit that may evolve in time, but whose segmentation within the evolution is unclear:

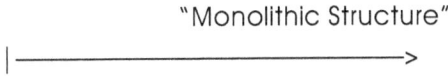

"Monolithic Structure"

|————————————————————>

Whatever progression that happens also acts to mask (hide) its changes, substituting sameness for marked intervals. The movie resembles the structure of a gestalt shape where the entire work can be grasped instantly. Expectations, chronological development, etc. are established instantly by this structure, allowing for the creation of surprise by breaking the structure.

These structures are simply points of a progression away from regularly marked time. The monolitic structure resembles the form of the steady-state work, and can be considered a diagram of that structure.

MODULARITY

Modularity is a fundamental part of movies: each frame is, at heart, a modular part of the whole, composed of still smaller modules, the pixels (or grains) themselves.

The concept of modularity is fundamental to structure. It exists at two levels of form: the individual, modular unity, and the structure created by the grouping of these modular units.

Each segment (short movie) is both a complete piece, composed in itself, and a component of a larger work whose dimensions and form are variable.

The creation and assembly of movies from smaller, internally complete and independent modules produces variable movies. This conception of modularity in the fabrication of movies is both serial (in the sense used by Umberto Eco) and montage-like (as in Sergei Eisenstein's theories).

EDITING

the question is not

        "to cut or not to cut"

but rather

        "when to cut"

All movies implicitly involve editing, even if it is elided in the continuous loop, since by presenting a work that chooses not to edit requires the potential "to cut" even if it only appears as the beginning or ending of the particular presentation of the work itself.

The editing of a movie determines its tempo, the sense of time a viewer has while watching it, and the meaning of the whole. Because all movies are edited (even those composed of a single shot) the presence or absence of an edit at any given point in the movie has significance for the meaning of the whole. The absence of edits during the long takes of David Lynch's Blue Velvet, most especially during the voyeuristic closet sequence, are significant because they draw attention to the voyeurism that the audience engages in while watching those scenes in this movie. In contrast, the speed, rhythm and superimpositions of the editing at the end of Dziga Vertov's Man with a Movie Camera provide a climax to the structure of the movie while reiterating its central themes.

KULESHOV EFFECT

In the late 1910's and early 1920's, Pudovkin, a Soviet film-maker and teacher performed a number of experiments where he would re-edit existing footage and then show the results to audiences, asking about the bits of film they saw. The most famous of these experiments involved an actor named Kuleshov whose expressionless face was juxtaposed through editing with a series of different images. Each time the audience is said to have responded differently, believing the actor's expression changed with each new combination. This mythical performance has become known as the basis for Soviet Montage, and is known as the Kuleshov Effect.

We can understand the significance of the experiment through Sergei Eisenstein's theorization and systematic explanation of Montage where the Kuleshov Effect stands as the pivotal break-through that enabled Eisenstein's own theories to develop. His theorization of Montage is based on the fact that the audience understood the meaning of Kuleshov's expression, not though his performance, but through the context provided by the other shots that accompanied Kuleshov.

Eisenstein ignores a key fact about this experiment in creating his montage theory by argue that editing should be understood linguistically: that every interpretation of Kuleshov's expression resulted from the audience's invention of a story to accompany the images shown. Kuleshov and a bowl of soup—he is hungry. Kuleshov and a graveyard—he is sad. Each of these interpretations implies something more than a linguistic use of images, (Eisenstein was, after all, guided by ideas imported from Japanese and Kabuki theater), they imply that the audience is understanding these shots in narrative terms, and are inventing a story that provides the emotional meaning for the imagery.

This narrative dimension is absent from discussions of the Kuleshov Effect, when it is discussed at all.

An alternative to Eisenstein's proto-montage understanding of the Kuleshov Effect is one that prioritizes the audience's narrative invention in relation to the shots combined through editing. With the addition of sound, it becomes possible to create situations where the viewers will "see" a "story," even though the actual narrative may be nothing more than suggested lines and some recurring people from shot or sequence to sequence. The appearance of "story" in such a movie would be entirely a construction of the audience, predicted by the Kuleshov Effect. The footage in such a film could be of any type so long as it was arranged relative to the narration. The viewers will create a synchronous continuity in-between the shots and in relation to the narrative simply because they are presented together. A number of different movies exploit this possibility: India Song, The Grapedealer's Daughter, Celine et Julie vont en Bateau, and my own She, my memory all approach this issue.

EISENSTEIN'S MONTAGE

Eisenstein's theory of montage* depends on the level of importance given to the images' content:

metric	rhythmic	tonal	overtonal	intellectual

————	————————	————————	————————	
low		(increasing levels of importance)		great
(visual)				(linguistic)

As the importance of the image's contents increases, it begins to contribute to, and then determine, the montage sequence's construction. Each stage in this scale includes the less complex forms as part of its structure.

> The metric and rhythmic montages treat the montage sequence musically, creating patterns and effects through the visual tempo of the editing.

> The intellectual montage approaches the assembly of the sequence in a linguistic fashion, as if each image were also a word.

* For a more complete discussion, see Sergei Eisenstein, "Methods of Montage" in Film Form.

JUMP CUTS

The jump cut was invented by Jean-Luc Godard in Breath-less. The construction is very simple. Because the action of a long take is continuous (by definition), with the staging and camera work acting to segment the scene through movement and re-framing, continuity editing becomes impossible.

But when a long take is condenses to only those portions that have significance for a specific scene, the result is the jump cut. The editing 'jumps' from point to point in the scene without concern for the relationships of continuity editing. This effect shat-ters the illusions created by long takes that the world in the realist drama is a continuous, independent fiction and not a product of illusionistic devices.

GRAPHIC MATCH

Editing based on graphic matches makes use of similar visual shapes in succeeding shots to present a sequence where the similar appearances serve to link different shots.

Screen position

Part of the process of graphic matches is editing by the screen position of the image's subject matter; this can be further elaborated when we recognize that it is the point on screen the audience is looking at immediately before and immediately after a cut that determines how smoothly the transition happens. When the editing changes images at a cut, but the arrangement of the screen positions the subject in the same position in both shots, the edit appears seamless.

This technique functions most clearly and directly when editing non-dramatic (especially abstract) footage, because the primary concern is the visual connection between images.

At the same time, this method offers the possibility for creating contrast and conflict between edits through a conscious mismatch of images. (Eisenstein's conflict dialectic depends on this mis-match.)

INTERLACING

Sample interlacing of two shots.

Interlacing takes the form of a flicker or pulse at the moment of shot change. It is a variety of "shot" transitions that imitates the decompression artifacts occasionally appearing in some poorly compressed .mpeg files. The frame count from one side of the structure to the other is similar to example above.

The insertion of these forms through the editing imitates a **glitch** that fragments the edit, but elides the actual "cut" as such: instead of cutting, pulsating flash-frames creates a transition from one shot to another, removing the straight cut as such. It usually lasts less than 1 second. It is most effective when kept as brief as possible since it otherwise starts to become rhythmic or metric montage.

PROJECTION

Projection Speed = Frame Change Rate

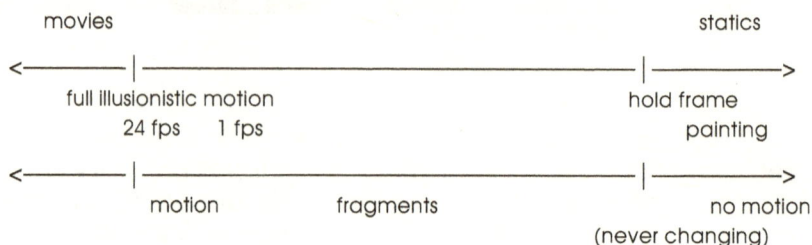

```
movies                                              statics

<————— | ——————————————————— | —————>
     full illusionistic motion            hold frame
        24 fps    1 fps                     painting

<————— | ——————————————————— | —————>
          motion        fragments          no motion
                                       (never changing)
```

A slide carousel changing frame every 5-30 seconds is identical to a movie that changes the image every x seconds.

Once we get below the 1 fps threshold, the images
appear with varying degrees of motion—starting
as fragments, then as motion in real time.

Both movies and statics can be understood in the same terms.

A painting only becomes visible through reflected
light produced from a projecting source. These pictures do change over time, but at a rate much
slower than real time.

Thus, the projector can be reduced to these elements:

the light beam (or electron beam)
the strobing device

The projector in this conception is a device allowing the appearance of motion in an image (even if there is no apparent motion in
real time). Some newer technologies can work as combinations of
projector and screen where each pixel becomes both a projector
and a screen (as in LCD screens). The "strobing device" in this
framework creates the projector's frame change rate.

For film, these three components are clearly separated; in video they are not. The TV builds the light source and strobing device are part of the screen itself, with the image (literally) embedded in this technology.

All light sources used as projectors (including the Sun) have a frame change rate (for the Sun it would be the period from sunrise to sunset), this is a constant for all light sources, even if its rate is only measured at speeds not visible in real time.

Modifications to the projector result in dramatically different kinds of movie.

The reason we can understand both movies and statics in the same ways is that the static is only a static because we are incapable of watching it change in real time, even though change is happening continuously.

The light that enables us to see the work is the common denominator between the movie and the static.

There are two kinds of projection:

reflective

emitive

Reflective projection bounces light back to the viewer.

Emitive projection produces the light seen by the viewer. This variety of projection most commonly involves the combination of projector and screen into a single unit: for example, TV.

The difference between one kind of projection and the other lies in the projection's source of the light—whether or not it originates on the screen's surface.

PROJECTOR-SCREEN RELATIONSHIPS

The relationship of projector-image-screen is variable. In the most common examples, the projector, the image and the screen are all part of the same device (TV, computer monitor); however this construction is not necessarily the case, since it is possible to imagine situations where these components are separated:

projector/image/screen   (TV, movieola, light box, etc.)

projector/image + screen   (projected film/video)

These first two varieties are familiar from everyday experience, but they are not the only potentials:

projector + image/screen   (painting, stained glass, etc.)

projector + image + screen

In the case of the **projector + image/screen** construction, the screen for the image also contains the image itself, and any motion that may appear must be a feature of the image's form rather than a result of a frame change rate replacing one image by another. All reflective artwork falls into this category.

The **projector + image + screen** is a potential that is logically consistent with this construction, but the specifics and dynamic of what such a construction might be is unknown.

SCREEN

The screen is the surface where the image appears. There are three kinds of possible surface:

transparent

translucent

opaque

transparent screens allow the light to pass through them without showing a very obvious image; a pane of transparent glass is an example

translucent screens allow light to pass through them, and depending on the degree of translucence, they may also include features of the environment visible through them. Smoke, fog and steam are vanities of translucent screens, as are rear projection screens.

opaque screens do not allow visible light to pass through them, and instead reflect the light projected onto them

Each type of screen surface interacts with the projection in different ways. Depending on what kind of screen a specific projection uses, the result will vary dramatically. These descriptions apply in all cases, whether the screen is a flat surface or a three dimensional object.

Screens are one of two general types:

fixed

variable

Fixed screens remain the same for the duration of the projection.

Variable screens change shape during the projection, making even movies that do not change in real time, or have very slow frame change rates much more visually active.

Screens can also be:

2D (flat)   or   **3D** (physical form)

solid   or   **permeable**

And, depending on where the projector goes, there are two more variations on the screen:

front projection

rear projection

2D screens do not necessarily have to correspond to the aspect ratio of the image.

No screens necessarily has to be the same size as the projected image; they can be larger or smaller. Anything can potentially become a screen. The significance of the screen comes from its relationship to the movie it supports.

Under most typical circumstances, the screen is hidden in the same ways that all parts of the technology of movies is hidden; so as not to interfere with the illusion it presents.

It is also possible to combine elements within a single projection, so it includes 2D and 3D elements.

SHAPED SCREENS

Beyond the obvious shaped screens that match the aspect ratio of the frame, screens can also be specially constructed to create particular effects and appearances that are not standard for movies:

irregular geometric shapes
organic shapes
domes, balls or other three-dimensional forms
etc.

Projecting movies onto objects can transform movies into site-specific works or can be used to animate surfaces in composite works that incorporate sculpture and performance into the final work.

However, screens of this type are no different than the more common variety, and the same potentials apply to them.

STROBE-BASED MOVIES

While all motion is an effect of a strobing light, in the strobe-based movie the image is actually printed onto the screen (rather than being a separate object), and the light source is simply a strobe light. The appearance of motion results from the image presenting a series of distortions that when seen quickly via a strobe light become apparent motion.

The physical design of the image used is a significant factor in its activation by the strobe. A movie of this type subverts all our expectations of both motion and stasis in the world around us.

I call these works "strobe-effect movies."

This is an example titled Village 3. The "flames" on the left part of the frame will appear to animate with a properly set strobe light.

These movies will appear to be a static when viewed without a strobe light. The image is animated through the movements of the viewer's eyes, and their cognitive adjustments between pulses. The greater the movement of the viewer, the greater the movement of the image.

Larger prints will have a more powerful effect than small prints because the visual effect (a close relative of painterly motion*) requires space to produce the strongest effect.

As with painterly motion, the appearance of movement depends of cognitive processes; the most effective movies thus work with realist imagery the audience can immediately recognize and where they have an already established understanding of the motion encountered in reality looks like. (This is the overlap with painterly motion.) Spatial discontinuities (multiple vanishing points, etc.) create a similar effect.

* Betancourt, Michael. "Motion Perception in Movies and Painting: Towards a New Kinetic Art," in CTheory, October 21, 2002.

SELF-REFERENCE

Brancusi's photography is a model for making work that is self-referential, but not "about" photography in the way most Modernist work is. The self-referential part of the image takes the form of the "flaws" in conventional photographs: finger prints, glare, dirt, dust, but has a different character than the appearance of these same things in the basal-formal film work. Their presence is incidental to the image, but they serve as a reminder that the image is a photograph.

A similar effect is possible in any medium: allow the errors and mistakes to remain in the final work as signifiers of its particular basis. These signifiers may be simulated to create the effects of being a different medium than reality. The comparison and contrast between two distinct media (one simulating the other) allows for a consideration of the nature of those media as such.

Foregrounding the "material" technology is a "newer" kind of transparency: the transparency of self-evident construction (a common feature of art since the 1960s). This was not the historical purpose of self-reference, but it is one of its effects as the audience accepts the self-reference as a formal device/effect.

INTENTIONS

The Intentional Fallacy is a concept that provides a framework for thinking about interpretation. The thesis of this article is very simple: that the intention of the artist is neither available nor desirable as a standard for judging the success of a work of art.

A fairly common belief among art-involved people is the idea that what determines something being "art" is a matter of intention: if the artist intended it to be art, it would be. However, as a consideration of The Intentional Fallacy shows, this specific belief cannot provide any formal basis for understanding the nature of art.

The Intentional Fallacy was invented in the 1950s by philosophers W. K. Wimsatt and Monroe C. Beardsley.* Their argument is concerned only with the criticism of poetry, but their logic applies equally well to any form of criticism, thus it is relevant to all art that involves interpretation.

Their argument is based on the idea of three kinds of "evidence" used in creating interpretations:

> (1) **Internal evidence.** This type of "evidence" comes from our historical knowledge and experience with the kind of art being interpreted: its forms, traditions, contextual references, and would also include the way it is exhibited, where, when and by whom. This information is internal to the type (or genre) of art that is being examined. Obviously, this also includes those things physically present to the work itself. This kind of evidence is what is present as fact.

> (2) **External evidence.** This is the private or idiosyncratic information that is not actually part of the work: these are the statements made privately or published in journals, in conversations, e-mail, etc that concern why the artist made the work—reasons external to the fact of the work in itself. Evidence of this type is directly concerned with what the artist may have intended to do even or especially when it is not apparent from the work itself.

*W. K. Wimsatt, Jr. and M. C. Beardsley, "The Intentional Fallacy" in Essays in Modern Literary Criticism, edited by Ray B. West, Jr., published by Holt, Reinhart and Winston, 1962.

For example, a pair of lint balls exhibited as a sculpture would, be necessity, rely on intentional supports to convey their meaning, even though it would make no difference to the quality of the balls, their appearance, etc. Such meaning would be an intentional fallacy.

> (3) **Contextual evidence.** This kind of evidence concerns the meanings derived from the specific works relationship to other art made by this particular artist. It can be biographical, but does not necessarily mean it is a matter of intentional fallacy. The character of a work may be inflected based on the particulars of who does the work without necessarily characterizing it as an intentional fallacy.

When evaluating a work or an interpretation, it is useful to consider the kind of claims being made—whether they are primarily related to (1) or (2); this helps to evaluate the (3) evidence that is being presented. An artist or critic more concerned with (1) than (2) will employ (3) in a very different fashion than someone concerned with (2). This is a distinction that effects the way artist approach their work, and what kind of interpretations and understandings are available from encountering the work itself.

While the concept of The Intentional Fallacy is recognizably related to other Modernist criticism from the 1950s, it runs counter to both the dominant Modernism in art promoted by Clement Greenberg, and the wholly open forms (so-called readerly) of interpretation common to Post-Modernism: deconstruction, semiotics, etc. where the meanings found can be a variant of (2) based solely on the tastes of the critic. Careful attention to the problematics of intention and the uninformed interpretation of a work should be a concern of anyone making art.

Basing any variety of definition art on these intentions—characteristics unavailable in the work itself—reduces the category of "art" to the personal tastes of the gate-keeper (gallerist, curator, critic) in relation to whatever happens to be fashionable at the moment of exhibition. This effectively evacuates meaning from the definition of "art." Instead what we have is something contingent on the fickle desires of the moment; perhaps this is good, perhaps not—but it does result in support for an Institutional definition of art, removing the potential for agency from the artist working.

A rejection of such intentional fallacies does not necessarily mean a return to tradition—instead what it suggests is a close awareness of prior history and a specific kind of relationship between the artist and that history.

An argument could be made (at another time) that this type of relationship is already in effect to some extent in the "high" art world: history (and to a lesser extent theory) plays much the same role as traditions once did. History in this sense is not a matter of a "historical destiny" popular in modernism, nor is it necessarily the "a la carte" menu of forms and stylistic markers popular with Post-Modernism, but offers a third option: a matrix of potentials that describe a field of activity. Investigations of what would formally constitute these potentials then becomes a significant activity since to identify them would serve to clarify for the artists working with a given medium what is possible.

SUBJECTIVITY

As The Intentional Fallacy suggests, the idea of subjectivity is deeply problematic for any kind of interpretation. There is a tendency to accept the claims made by artists for their work, even when the work quite clearly and visibly contradicts those claims.

Subjective processes are inevitable. However, they also present a danger for anyone making anything: that the resulting work does not actually do/say what the person making it thinks it does or should do. For this reason, entirely subjective explorations do not usually appear in my work: it is very difficult to communicate them (if not impossible in some cases) and can very easily produce work like this:

Abstract Film

(person standing, facing camera)
"I'm thinking about this here."
(points to head)

The trouble with making entirely and only subjective works is: there is very little space left over for the audience.

This is not to say that subjectivity can or even should be avoided, only that it should not be the sole guiding principle for a movie. The Intentional Fallacy applies equally to the creative and productive process of making work as it does to interpretation. Working with the issues of how an audience would encounter a work in mind can help make the interpretation of that work clearer and more direct.

FASCINATION

I believe fascination is one of the essential elements in art. Without it, an artwork is unable to hold interest long enough for it to form meanings.

Fascination related to our response to the work, quite apart from any emotional response it may provoke. It is what keeps us looking even if we decide we don't want to. It is partially cultural, partially psychological-biological, but is not exclusively tied to subject matter or realism: abstract art must have this or else there is nothing.

THE ENTERTAINER

The Entertainer is the primary producer for mass-market driven, consumer-oriented, bottom-line culture where expenses and cost are always weighed against human life. There is no place in entertainment for questions of quality—the only factor that matters is the bottom-line: net and gross profits.

Thus the underlying distinction between the work of the entertainer and the artist is what determines the success or failure of the outcome: questions of quality, or questions of profit.

Entertainment is always judged by the conditions of kitsch, rather than questions of aesthetics. It will continuously search for novelty in both form and approach, but will insist on its own values when confronting the finished work. Thus, artists must be careful when dealing with the mass-media entertainment conglomerate: entertainment exists to nullify the difficult because bottom-line profits require the work be accessible, and reach as large an audience as possible—in order to maximize profits.

This is not to say that artists should give their work away, or that they ought to avoid selling their work: only that there are dangers to the quality of the work when the issue of profits are allowed to be the determining factor for success or failure.

PRACTICE

a note

I chose the movies discussed in this section because they are the ones I believe are important for the later development of the theory; what is visible here is a gradual change from movies built around verbal language to movies that rely more heavily on visual means to create their meaning and effects.

This change from verbal to visual comes from successful experiments that made it possible to abandon verbal language (the "this means this" of some early movies) for a visual language not tied to representation, or to commercial, narrative form.

THE STORY OF IT

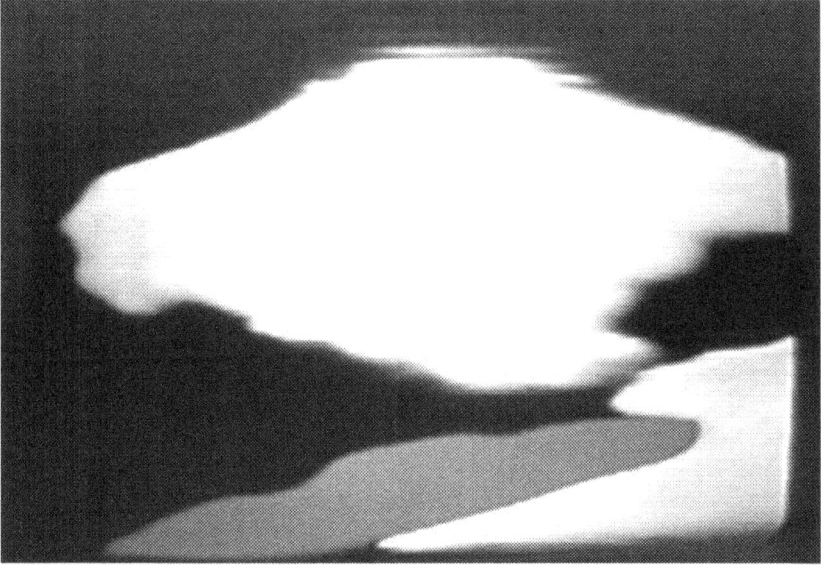

The Story of It was performed by Mary Betancourt and Ben Fried.

This story grew out from a simple deconstructive realization about the true nature of pronouns: that the pro of pronouns stands for professional, as with professional sports—prosports. The rest of the story followed logically and inevitably from this simple premise.

It is the soundtrack for a short film of the same title, currently in distribution through Canyon Cinema.

It was a small word, and was often beaten up and used by much larger words like Insanity and Dogma. For many years It suffered abuse by them, until it finally escaped and became one of the truly powerful words, the professional nouns. It took its place among the other pronouns, each group headed by important words like He, She, You, They, and of course, I at the annual pronoun ball, where, it is rumored, all the nouns and pronouns gather every year to elect a new watchword to govern the secret congress of words—which, as you know, is the way new words are made from the union of old words. It was content and happy at the ball, in its new-found prestige, as one of the few personal pronouns of the language.

And for a while It was complacent in its new-found recognition.

Overtime, It began to realize its potential to confuse and confound things, destroying meaning in the process. At first, It misused this power, working against having any meaning at all, but its revolt did It more harm than it did it anything else, making It into a word that referred to indefinite things, and without any identity at all.

It, on learning this, became worried that one day it would lose all personality and become indefinite—meaningless by itself—something it didn't want. It was a form of mid-life crisis for It. However, it resolved this crisis by deciding that it was not its' problem, but that of other words; It decided that it was better than all that, and didn't need to concern itself with other words grammar.

And so It went on to become the most powerful word of all, since, in the final analysis, it only refers to it and to nothing else.

The combination of such a simple, absurd parody of a children's story with abstract imagery produced with video feedback was the dialectical opposition of all the early movies: the opposition and commingling of verbal and visual languages.

A SELF-REFERENTIAL FILM IN 30 SENTENCES

This movie was suggested by Douglas Hofstadter's thoughts about self-reference.

This is the first sentence in a self-referential film about self-reference.

This is the second sentence, which comes after the first and is followed by the third, but has very little to do with it.

In this, the third sentence, the main character is mentioned.

In the fourth sentence, the main character's name is revealed to be Joe.

Joe gets drunk on a fifth in the fifth sentence.

The sixth sentence concerns the day after Joe got drunk in the fifth on a fifth.

The seventh sentence wonders what the fifth and sixth refer to.

The eighth sentence is confused.

The ninth sentence wonders about how useful self-reference is as the main content, and whether or not self-reference can actually be a functional method for story-telling, and ultimately gets back to the main character, Joe.

Joe, in the tenth sentence, goes to school.

That school is described as being like a prison in the eleventh sentence.

While there, Joe contemplates the Zen Proverb, "This sentence no verb." in the twelfth sentence.

The thirteenth sentence is omitted because it is unlucky.

The fourteenth sentence continues the contemplation.

"This sentence no verb." is the next sentence.

This sentence no verb.

Now is the time for a meaningless pause, having nothing to do with anything.

That.

This is the sentence that comes after that.

This sentence is the last sentence, but it also comes earlier.

The twenty-first sentence returns to Joe, who is inactive, trapped inside the Zen Proverb.

The problem with self-reference is that every sentence must refer to itself, as is the case when this sentence says what it says again, that is, the problem with self-reference is that every sentence must refer to itself.

That sentence, unlike this one, is very long.

Joe goes home in this sentence.

This is the twenty-fourth sentence out of thirty.

This is the twenty-fifth sentence, which means there are five left.

In the twenty-seventh sentence, we learn that the twenty-fourth and -fifth sentences were lying.

This sentence isn't sure if it should trust #27.

This is the antepenultimate sentence.

This is the penultimate sentence.

This sentence is the last sentence, but it also comes earlier.

Designs from the production of a self-referential film in 30 sentences .

storyboard

camera set-up

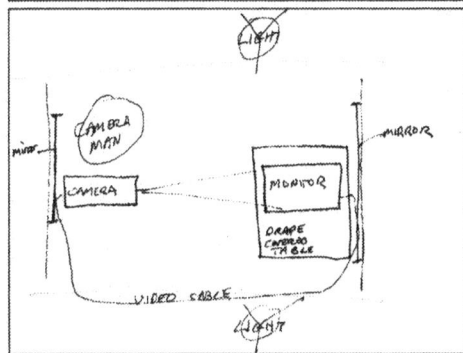

A self-referential film in 30 sentences was shot in one day in March '94, preceded by a year of notes, thoughts, conversations, It was edited and a print first seen in May '94. I wanted to make a summation of my nervous system, historical beliefs and aesthetic ideas. I was thinking about a complex of parody, quotation and so-lipsism in which the absurdity of "pure" film space and time would appear. The space begins with video feeback and gradually zooms out to reveal the reference-into-depth that is inherent in all feedback systems: the infinite regression of image within image.

The film is an apparently continuous zoom out of and into a

portable video screen. It was shot with a fixed camera placed on one side of an 8-foot space. The seamless space is interrupted by several mirrors which reflect into each other the filming process and the monitor itself, forming a second-level of feedback in the physical world. The sentences of the title scroll up the image, relating to each other and to the zoom, at times controlling the pauses and setting the pace for the film as a whole. They are interrupted once by a pause lasting some seconds. The silence of these moving words is the silence of Zen contemplation, the absence of anything but itself as a whole subject. The is the quiet of solipsism into which the sentences about sentences and the feedback must ultimately settle.

As this description shows, a self-referential film in 30 sentences is a parody of Michael Snow's film Wavelength.

THINGS

Things was the first movie I created that could be broken into modular units, even though it was not. The structure of the film was punctuated with brief connecting images that served to separate each section of the text/narration. This formal device would eventually break the movie into separate parts (modules) whose arrangement could then be easily adjusted, based on their relationship to the whole.

THIS IS A FILM ABOUT NOTHING.

That is to say

It has no subject,

Or,

Its subject is its lack of subject.

Normally, film has a subject.

This film does,

But it doesn't,

Because Nothing is the subject.

If Nothing is Something,

Then the film is getting confused.

[image punctuation]

There is an expression

"Something for Nothing."

It has Nothing to do with Anything.

Many times people get

"Nothing for Something."

It isn't Anything at all.

Anything and Something are

Not Nothing,

But Nothing is Something,

It can be Anything.

NOTHING IS CONFUSING.

So is Everything, but
                    Anything can be confusing.
                    If you know
                              Everything
                    You'll be alright.

[image punctuation]

Nothing isn't Anything,
                         But it is Something.
                                   Nothing and Anything
                         Are both things
                         But they're not
                                   Everything.
              Can Nothing
              Be Nothing?

              THINGS ARE STRANGE.

      The most visible feature of this movie is its text has the potential to continue indefinitely. What it presents is a process of thinking about "nothing" as an actual value that a movie could have, and the paradoxes that result because it is a value representing the absence of value.

      The arrangement of the text is significant since it allows an alternative series of readings, using the position of the text, rather than the grammatical sentences.

POST FILM

Most "experimental" work can easily be reduced to a set of conventions that serve to identify and describe the genre as such. Listings of this type, whether for a genre, or as the particular "rules" for a single movie, can provide guidelines that make the actual work of putting the movie together much easier because they provide a stable reference, independent of subjective concerns, doubts, etc. that may arise while making the movie.

Post Film was created from such a listing for the genre of video art, making it a movie-manifesto of sorts, standing against those conventions and objecting to the genre "art film" as it is conventionally conceived.

This is an art film.

Because this is an art film it is intellectual, not emotional.

Because this is an art film it must use self-reference a lot.

Because this is an art film it must use text on screen.

Because this is an art film it must repeat things.

Because this is an art film it must annoy the audience.

Because this is an art film it must be too long for the idea.

This is not an art film.

ACTION MOVIE

This movie was produced on a residency at the Experimental Television Center in Owego, NY during the spring of 1996. It was my first opportunity to test some theoretical propositions about movies; the experience clarified many issues and prompted the reconsideration of the physical technology itself that created divisions into: camera / image(base) / editing / projector / screen / sound.

It was my first attempt to make a movie based solely on visual language; because it was a failure, making it "work" required the addition of a series of short statements, that taken as a whole form a simple narrative:

Which side of the bed is the wrong side?

If you're not yourself today, the who are you?

If you run out of time, are you timeless?

Do you have to be a carnation to get reincarnated?

PORTRAIT FILM

This script was narrated/revised by Brad Blank.

This film has no plan, no architecture but for a through-line of the black frame/color image.

All the rest is just playing, me with bits of images which seemed right to make and even more right to assemble together.

There was originally a plan, but it was wrong.

This film is to be personal and I don't want to work with a plan in mind. That comes later, sometimes much later, and so for the film to have a plan would be for it to fail.

So, instead, all I'm doing is putting bits and pieces together and hoping that in the end, "yes, Jim, the end" they'll all make some sort of sense, at least to me.

This film will (hopefully) not be a diary "yes, Anne," or a confessional, "Padre," but rather something, something, I know not what.

The sense of Deja Vu hangs all over it.

P. Adams Sitney writes in Visionary Film that artists are supposed to make personal statements in their work (the assumption here is about being subjective). What logically follows from this claim is that if an work does not make a personal statement, then it is not art, and the person making it is not an artist. It is a claim that makes the dismissal of art, artists, and anything connected to them almost inevitable.

I wrote the original script for this movie, then asked the performer to make additions and changes suggested to him by that script. This process was an experiment in breaking the framework presented by Sitney's prescriptions.

The images created for this film were derived from the language commonly used to talk about "artist's work": being able to see the hand of the artist in the final product.

POSTCARD FILM

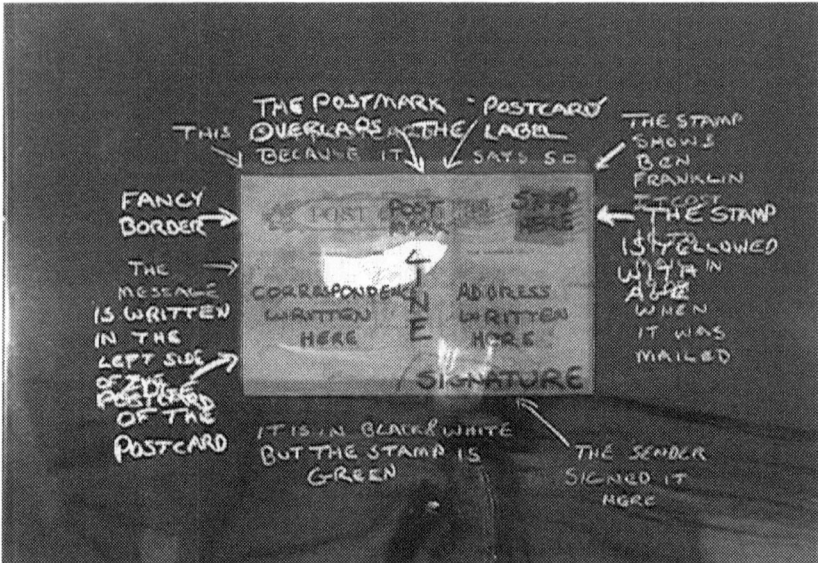

Postcard Film presents a series of transparent overlays of handwritten commentary on an antique postcard of a small boat being drawn up on a sandy beach. The choice of this image offered me the possibility for visually "unloading" verbal language as a progressively more constraining and obscuring means for conveying the content of a movie.

Each successive layer of text overwrites the earlier layers, and in the process prevents the viewer from being able to read more than an increasingly small portion of the contents. This process changes the visual words into an illegible visual scrawl over the duration of the movie.

UNSEEN FILM SUBSTITUTION
ABECEDARIUM: U

The Abecedarium was an experimental "sketch book" that allowed the exploration of topics and issues related to experimental film. It was organized around the idea of a children's alphabet primer: 26 sections, one for each letter.

This modular movie was made from a series of short pieces. Although unfinished, it clarified many aesthetic and structural principles that are at work in later movies.

The audience will substitute the memory of

a film they saw and enjoyed for

this portion of the program.

Unseen Film Substitution is an example of a conceptual movie, like conceptual art, the emphasis is on the idea, rather than on exists physically. Instead, it is a set of instructions which the audience is encouraged to consider as if they could actually perform them.

VICTIMS

Victims was performed by Tom Gormley, with vintage radio news coverage of the JFK assassination, and video of the Rodney King beating rephotographed off a TV screen in extreme close-up.

> Alright, it's a simple situation. This is how it works: Victims victimized by victimizers will victimize their victimizers, making the victims into the victimizers who now victimize the victimizers because they were victims. However, this perpetuates the victimizer-victim relationship because the victims, now victimizers, victimize those who were victimizers, creating new victims who will victimize again because they were victimized; this victimization of victimizers makes more victims who will only live to victimize again. Victims victimizing victimizers, now victims victimized who victimize other victim-victimizers victimize still more victimizer-victims victimized by victimization.

It was a return to text-based movies, but with a key difference: the visual and the verbal were not in direct opposition.

ILLUMINATION

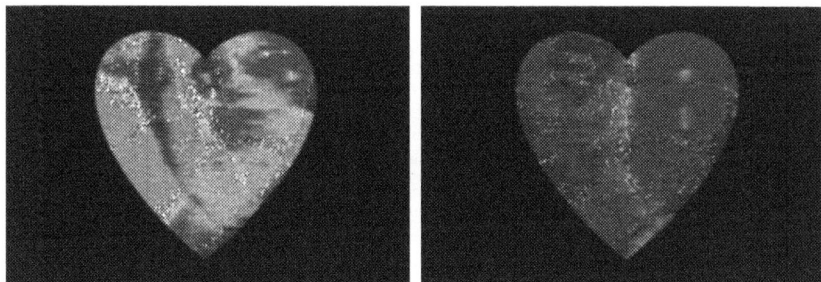

"Sergei Eisenstein was the first to study extensively the relation of image (in film) and language. A pioneer in the creation of the 'montage theory,' he also engaged in research in Chinese characters and analyzed the ideographic elements in detail; his theory of montage, in fact, developed out of this work. As an example (though not necessarily one of Eisenstein's), the combination of the word SUN and the word MOON makes the word ILLUMINATION."

—Takahiko Iimura, a quotation from his essay,
"Visuality in the Structure of the Japanese Language"

This movie was prepared specifically for a show whole theme was love and sex. I chose this quotation for two reasons, both obliquely connected to this theme: in Japanese, when two characters combine to create a new meaning, it is called "intercourse," and the kind of visual transformation that happens in it is similar to the kind of combination Iimura describes in his essay as a natural property of movies.

Illumination explores the ability of DV to visualize the kind of transformation Iimura describes: the shift from one visual representation to another, with meaning changing as well. The movie presents a progression of images that move between abstraction and representation: the shift is from blocks of color arranged into a heart-shape into a face that then decomposes into a network of cracks and lines.

It was the first suggestion that speed ramping DV in a computer would cause the fields to separate into visible parts of the movie, and this change would create the potential form motion different and independent of whatever subject matter the video might contain.

NEW MOVIES

New Movies are modular. Each part of the group is an independently created and produced work whose place in the whole was determined later. As a result, the movies that comprise any New Movie program can be shown singly or as part of the whole.

However, the collection called New Movies (2001) have a series of features and concerns in common. They were all produced in 2001; each piece works towards a unitary gestalt form by minimizing or eliding the appearance of editing (they are all heavily edited); each piece is the product of specific transformations applied to a limited amount of video, and their motion emerges from the technology and processing. In several cases, the source materials were still images.

New Movies (2001) focused on the potentials of DV, in particular the properties of resolution changes and compression codecs for creating imagery and motion not present in the original footage.

New Movies (2002) developed issues of editing and synchronization between image, rhythm and music I specifically composed for use in my movies.

New Movies (2001) and New Movies (2002) are mirror images of each other: both are specific experiments and explorations in the traditions of abstract film practice. New Movies (2001) approaches these issues from the side of VJ culture using the night club with its distracted contemplation. The formal requirements of work done and shown in a setting where the audience watches, but not in the way they do in a theater, makes very particular demands on what can be done with the movie. To a large extent, work meant to be screened this fall falls victim to the demands of its presentation.

In contrast to this viewing situation is the classical abstract film explored in New Movies (2002). These movies explore this classical tradition (a form that produced the VJ tradition in the popular forms of abstraction starting in the 1960s) that is meant to be screened in a theater with a captive, attentive audience who will watch the movie though from the beginning. There is a greater flexibility to these movies due to their being so completely contained in a specialized ("ideal") viewing environment.

These movies were made to explore and clarify the conditions and formal expectations an audience has when encountering abstract movies from either tradition. That the VJ and classical traditions are at cross purposes may be more a result of the specific viewing conditions than an aesthetic disagreement about form and technique.

I needed New Movies (2001) and New Movies (2002) to clarify these traditions and what relationship they have to each other for myself. These groups theoretically grounded my approach and working methods in a "living" tradition that only becomes apparent once you start attempting to participate. NM02 is closely modeled on the work of Oskar Fischinger, Len Lye and Hy Hirsch. Of the three, Hirsch was the greatest relevance since his work was not synchronized in the slavish fashion of Fischinger.

A certain flexibility in the audio-visual dynamic is important since it promotes counterpoint structures and, thus encourages a highly engaged audience.

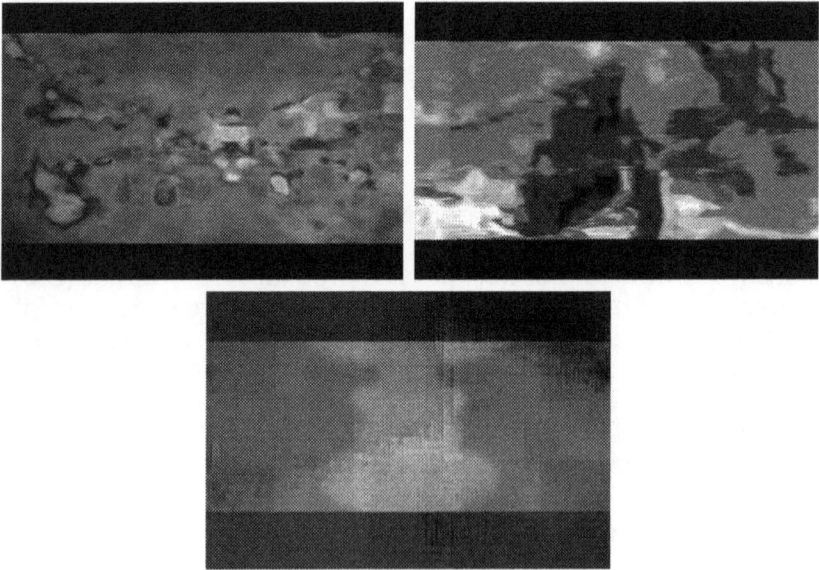

Still images from New Movies 2001.

SHE, MY MEMORY

Narrated and shot by Henry Rajan.

She, my memory is an experiment in collage and creating the effect of a story (including a plot). It was made from footage shot with a Sony CDMavica still camera that could also shoot short, low resolution .mpegs. The resulting footage, shot in India during December 2001 by Rajan, does not tell a story in itself, but by being reworked, edited and combined with appropriate narrative could create the effect of a story.

It was constructed from short narrated modules each approximately 60 to 90 seconds in length and linked either visually, verbally or both so the transition from one module to another is nearly invisible in the final construction.

She, my memory explores some of the personal contradictions, possessiveness, and authoritarian side of love that Proust wrote about:

> And I realized the impossibility which love comes up against. We imagine that it has as its object a being that can be laid down in front of us, enclosed within a body. Alas, it is the extension of that being to all the points in space and time that it has occupied and will occupy. If we do not possess its contact with this or that place, this or that hour, we do not possess that being. But we cannot touch all these points. If only they were indicated to us, we might perhaps contrive to reach them. But we grope for them without finding them. . . . We waste time on absurd clues and pass the truth without suspecting it.

—Marcel Proust, a la recherche du temps perdu

HAPPY PEOPLE

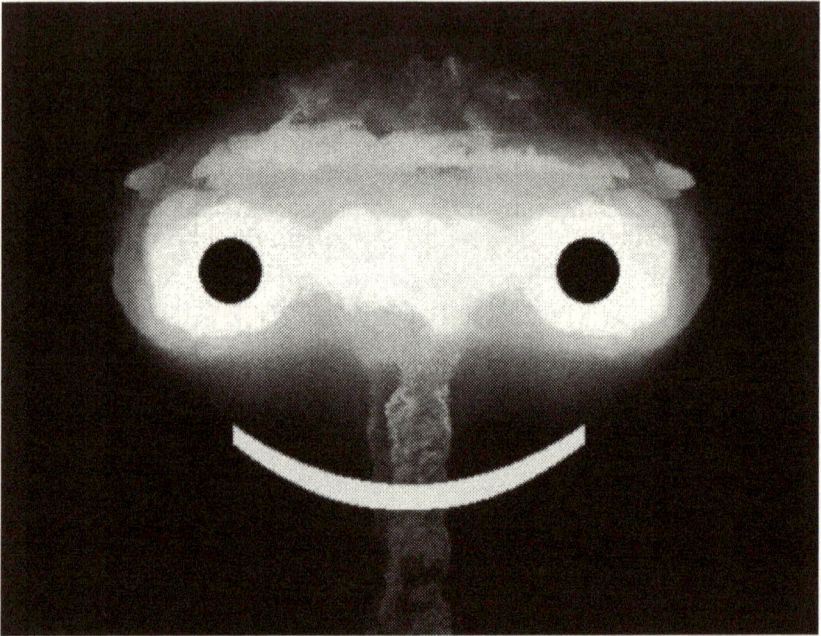

Happy People was performed by Henrietta Marco.

With so much emphasis on being happy these days, sooner or later we meet the Happy People. They're happy because they're taking prescription drugs that make them happy. It hides their depression about their lives. The space these Happy People inhabit isn't really theirs, it's just borrowed. But don't worry, be happy! They are.

Happy People is a continuous loop where two voices argue about being happy; one is happy and theother isn't. The image slowly changes color, cycling through the entire spectrum.

PRON

"PrOn" is a word used by the hacker community to talk about on-line porn. it references both the tendency of censorware to screen materia based on words and the move Tron that presented an artificial electronic "fantasy." PrOn plays with all these references to make a movie about sex, voyeurism and masturbation using materials from the Internet.

PrOn was an experiment prompted by work on Year that demonstrates the potential for the image-temporal matrix as a vehicle for more than just abstract imagery. Completed while Year was still in-progress, it influenced the final form of Year.

It is a layering of found materials brought on the residency and blended together, whose placement remains established and works with predetermined norms of visual language: the subject matter of each image. This kind of material is obvious, and while it raises issues/questions without resolving them, it does not add much to already existing discussions except in the form of non-dogmatic eye candy. (In itself useful, but insignificant.)

PrOn's structure is based on a realist variant of the **image-temporal matrix** where reiteration (sameness) processed and transformed creates visual variety from limited material.

This movie prompts specific considerations in relation to classical film theory: the questions of scopophilia and voyeurism.

Scopophilia is not some disconnected (sublimated) plea-sure-in-looking as film theory impunes. It is a dramatic, active activ-ity connected to sexual gratification that is the reason the voyeur's actions are unacceptable. It is a matter of what the "peeping tom" does while at the keyhole.

It we engage "voyeurism" but pretend the voyeur is a pas-sive looker, we deny the underlying action of this pathology, and create a situation where any viewing situation can be regarded as voyeuristic. It is the active quality of voyeurism that separates it from looking (or watching). We become aware of voyeuristic issues precisely because they are not part of our typical experience, and this is the thing that makes able to recognize voyeurism when we do encounter it.

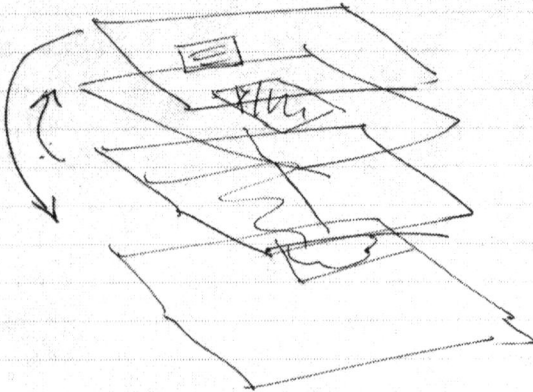

Production diagram describing the structure and development.

YEAR

Year is an attempt to explore and experience those things we do not normally notice because we are too busy. Because abstraction simply is, it has the potential to make us see the world differently. It makes use of both digital artifacts and analog processing effects to create abstract imagery by exploring our ability to visualize space and movement through color. Compression artifacts present us with a ready-made image of interpretation and memory, made visible by the technical properties of our technology. Digital signal decay is an almost inevitable consequence of working with compressed video, and its presence is magnified by successive generations of processing.

Portions of Year were also processed with analog machinery at the Experimental Television Center in Owego, New York, allowing me to draw together more than a decade of experiments with color, space, motion and perception.

There are twelve sequences of Year, which are organized around monthly birthdays of people I know. This connection gives a human dimension to an otherwise abstract work. In each sequence, I matched the mood, imagery and rhythm—to the person.

The individuality element provided a framework for the

structure and color choices in each sequence, and prompted the beginning epigraph from William Shakespeare's Henry the Fifth:

> we see which way the stream of time doth run
> and are enforced from our most quiet there by the
> rough current of occasion

Celebrations provide a conclusion to what has gone before while preparing for what is yet to come. They are an interruption of our routines, and make us aware of the ways most of the time our lifeworld is strictly limited to what we expect and anticipate.

The two variations on the visual space of Year depends on how color acts: a 3D version in stereo, and a flat version. The version we see is a result of how we watch the movie. In the flat version, we watch it as we would any movie, with the space appearing through traditional techniques of overlapping planes, color contrast and perspective. However, the other version uses Chromadepth™ glasses to produce a three-dimensional space based on color separation by wavelength of light—red is foreground and blue is background, with the rest of the spectrum falling in between.

The nature of video as a result of additive color mixing makes the spaces revealed by Chromadepth™ glasses especially brilliant and effective. The video technology complicates these spatial relationships, and new possibilities for presenting space through color appear as a result of video's way of creating color on screen. The movement between the Chromadepth™ spaces and traditional perspective in the 3D version allows me to animate the visual space in ways that are impossible with two dimensional media. This interplay between perspective and Chromadepth™ depends on color.

The spaces Year presents are in excess of what we might expect from this 3D technology in encounters with photographs for example. Because video creates its colors through the optical mixing of Red, Green, and Blue, the spaces we see with Chromadepth™—even when watching apparently flat, single-color, monochromatic sequences—open up what we would expect to be a "flat" space to hidden volumes. This is a new effect, previously unknown with Chromadepth™.

My realization that this kind of spatial visualization based purely on color and video's handling of it enabled me to make this movie. I have been in contact with American Paper Optics, the company that manufactures Chromadepth™, and they were un-aware that this kind of effect was possible with their technology. (In fact, they told me it wasn't possible.)

Our perceptions are more subtle, and our ability to distin-guish color variation is greater than we generally assume. The spa-tial variances that appear in Year's monochrome sections suggest a degree of color sensitivity in excess of what we experience in our everyday lives. This revelation about our sense of color becomes a metaphor in Year through its two variations: the unseen qualities of the people whose birthdays provide the basis for each sequence.

It is this shift from superficial appearance to complexity that prompted my decision to create Year so it can support two distinct versions: the 3D version is always present, implicit in the relation-ships of the flat version, and its appearance is a form of insight into the relationships and complexity of the everyday.

Chromadepth™ glasses provide a technical means for ev-eryone to have this encounter. Shifting to this visual understanding happens in the process of our viewing, from memory and familiarity with its content the rhythmic structure is a combinatory process made of variations on simple patterns. Each sequence is brief so we do not become tired by these structures. Like the people whose birthdays provide the framework for Year, familiarity brings an awareness of the depth and complexity that lies hidden.

TELEMETRY

     Telemetry originates with some specific potentials for visual form and structure implicit in Year: the image-temporal matrix, a formal device that is based around the recursion of feedback, but only when treated in an explicitly fractal manner in relation to time. Every moment of an image-matrix (when fully articulated as in the omega sequence) contains representations (echoes) of every other moment from that episode. It is a steady-state, atemporal construction where the only aspect missing is the dimension of motion, even though all the points of that movement are visible simultaneously.

     The evolution of the whole is both immanent and a product of the entire temporal development of the whole: this is the underlying paradox of the image-temporal matrix and those works deploying it.

     Telemetry is a documentary whose subject is those things that fall outside our direct perception. It adopts an abstract form precisely because what is represented has no direct physical form we can directly encounter. Instead our electronic intermediaries (the satellites and deep space probes) send back their observations as numerical data we interpr114et intellectually to understand what it is like in those places we cannot go, what those things we cannot see look like.

The exploration and study of the heavens begins in ancient times as a religious practice, but becomes in the age of science an empirical matter. The Sun is the electromagnetic and gravitational center to our solar system. Its radiation (visible and invisible) bathe our world and give it life.

Telemetry is composed of a short prelude based on a solar flare shot at the Lowell Observatory in October 1971, followed by 24 sections that begin with the Greek Alpha and end with Omega. These letters carry both scientific and mystical significance, as does any attempt to understand the heavens and our place in them.

Selected Filmography

1992 Archaeomodern

1994 The Story of It
A Self-Referential Film
          in 30 Sentences
Things
For/Fore/Four Father
Samizdat

1995 Post Film
Making OJ
Whitman Sampler

1996 Liar
Action Movie

1997 Abecedarium
Portrait Film
lime disease

1998 hide-and-seek
Postcard Film

2000 Found Film
Tache
Victims
(no title)
We Knowtice
Protect the Children
nu (parts 1-4)
Mile High Club
Strawberry
Water Under the
          Muybridge

2001 nu (parts 5-9)
Aurora
Study to be Quiet
Illumination
Abstrakt
Need
Squares for Breakfast
Tortured Corridor
Punch
Mushroom
Smile
5m8
913-7
Civis
RGB
17sfhjk
be1c
Semix

2002 nu (part 10)
Stille Nacht
Neon
Dodge
she, my memory
O Television
Look Out
          (he's got a knife)
Forces of Symmetry
Perspective

2003 PRON
Year

2004 W
Telemetry

APPENDIX

a note

The materials presented in this Appendix, while they are not theoretical, neither are they directly a part of the Practical application of these ideas. Instead, what this Appendix contains are related tools and conceptual works that are relevant to the aesthetic guiding the application and development of these experiments: these are the subjective aspects of working.

THE _____ MANIFESTO

M A N I F E S T O

Today, _____ itself is obsolete. In documenting art
on the basis of _____; we are human and true
for the sake of _____, _____ and
_____. At the crossroads of the lights, alert,
attentively awaiting _____.

If you find it futile and don't want to waste your time on a
_____ that means nothing, consider that here we
cast _____ on fertile ground. Here we have a right
to do some prospecting, for we have _____.
We are ghosts drunk on energy, we dig into _____.

We are a _____ as tropically abundant as
_____, which is the art of making
_____ established as _____ on a
canvas before our eyes, yet today the striving for
_____ in a work of art seems _____
to art. Art is a _____ concept, exalted as
_____, inexplicable as life, indefinable and
_____. The work of art comes into being
through the _____ of the elements.

The medium is as _____ as the artist. Essential only
is the forming, and because the medium is _____,
any _____ whatsoever will _____.

_____ is the name for such art.
_____ stands for freedom. _____
changes meaning with the change in the insight of those who
view it. Every artist must be allowed to mold a picture out of
_____. The _____ of natural elements
is _____ to a work of art. Instead, it is the
artist who _____ to produce _____,
in order to make a better art.

STATEMENT

To paraphrase John Cage:

We need to make movie, not films, videos, etc.

We need to make statics, not paintings, photographs, etc.

We need to make art, not money, fashion, or fame.

We need the right goals to make the next thing.

When we work to be famous, to be rich, etc. we do not do what is needed.

We need to do something, else then what are we doing?

We need to begin by saying "this is what has been done" so we can do something that has not been done.

What would this be?

---

2 historical phases:

(1) innovation/experiment/innovation
(2) mastery and synthesis

(1) is over and (2) has begun.

They are equal positions, each devalued by the other. Each position is antithetical to the other, working towards different, mutually exclusive goals. At the moment of transition from (1) to (2), a shift that may take 50 to 100 year, position (1) becomes the dominant approach even though it simply repeats earlier experiments and innovations, and (2) becomes the disruptive force, a position marginalized and whose significance is denied by those in position. In the nineteenth century these positions were reversed: (2) was dominant and (1) was called the avant-garde; this relationship had reversed by the 1940s.

The power relationship between these positions oscillates through time, each reversing the other. The interaction between positions (1) and (2) are based on whichever position is dominant, (not just in the art world, but in the culture as a whole), and in control of the systems of exhibition, criticism, etc.

MEDIA MYTHOS

After more than a century of gradual development we have arrived at a point in time where all our desires, interests, beliefs, and thoughts are carefully tallied and counted through polls and marketing analysis to better sell us anything that we might happen to have a passing fancy for. This situation has resulted in a simultaneous creation and destruction within our collective psyches. The past has become as much a closed world as it is a world before. The meaning which invested itself in all aspects of our arranged human world are now as meaningless as stones. We do not exist with the density of meaning which invested the worlds of our ancestors. This is what we have lost, destroyed by the need of manufacturing and consumption to always provide new goods, new services, even if these good and services are themselves unnecessary, or even wasteful, of our lives and our money. The goods are produced, so there must be a market for them, consumers willing and able to pass over their currency for whatever thing it is that is sold.

To make this transaction easier for us, the marketing and public relations industries—they are industries in more than metaphoric sense—have evolved. Their only purpose is to make us desire and act on our desire by purchasing what ever object happens to be their task of the moment to sell. Meaning must be lost in this process or else we might not buy; with meaning comes responsibility and a connection to the past, with its prohibitions against exactly the kind of spurious activity marketing and public relations use as the basis of their sales pitches. Marketing sells objects; public relations sells ideas. Both use the same techniques to encourage actions by their audiences.

Human beings, however, do not survive well without a constellation of meaning surrounding them, and where meaning is absent, it is created. The so-called "gang" and youth cultures—while containing an element of the marketing and public relations sales pitches (it is inevitable that both would attempt to evacuate meaning from these cultures)—are spontaneous developments of meaning against the attempts at erasure by the industries which are adopted and reused by these groups. That both cultures are produced primarily by youths is not accidental. It is the youths who most need to make connections to constellations of meaning because it is only through such connections that individuals build relationships to the world beyond their immediate self. Without such connections there can be no community since a community is embodied specifically by individuals with specific, clearly defined relationships. It is a circular arrangement by necessity.

What happens when the bonds between the past meanings and the present world are broken is quite simple: without myths, fables and religion to provide a series of psychological tropes, those objects and stories told through the media replace the mythological world. Scooby Doo replaces the trickster Coyote; Hellraiser replaces Inferno, creating a world without possibility of redemption, where the monstrous can only be defeated momentarily because they will inevitably return in sequels (to high profits).

Once there was a mythological world which found its partner in the minds of individuals, a fact noted by both Freud and Jung. But it is a fact that seems less and less physically present with each passing day because what once was part of the natural order is now unusual; the images of our consciousness are created and marketed by the media, and it is here that we find the images we once knew reborn, reformulated to become something different. Our psyches are filled with imagery of media: electronic, fleeting, unreal, and unnatural. It is this which has become the source for our new myth world.

TECHNOLOGY / SEX

Digital Combinations

An art of movies not based on narrative, whose content is purely digital: the pulsing of data and whose form subsumes the history of painting into itself.

Begin with the encodings, whose sexualized contents—a lover's kiss, sex, etc.—becomes distant, yet ever-present. Translate this to the pulsations of color, the rhythm of oscillations moving in/out, gliding across and through: the mirroring of self in other.

Fractal patterns into depth becoming mirrors for the physical. Interchange of data as a sexual process: Electrical plugs and sockets are called "male" and "female."

FOUR-LETTER WORDS

This is a script-description for a movie I decided not to make. It is an important transitional piece between the text-based movies and the visual ones. It suggests a transformation of language into image.

Like most movie-ideas, this one is little more than a set of instructions for a procedure that would result in a movie, but without providing enough particulars to delineate what the completed work would actually be like. This lack of specific detail is derived from both the lacunae in conceptual art's instructions, and, the earlier instructions provided by Marcel Duchamp's various collections of notes.

(1996)

black out every 4 letter word in a Gideon Bible

(note: **HOLY** is four letters long)

_____

use a variety of colors: some should be highlighted, other obliterated, some in-between

the idea is to get an interesting visual pattern to pixellate the screen

_____

Don't just shoot it on 1s.

Compose a 'score' of frame #s and then, later, add music in counterpoint to the rhythms of the image track

STROBE-EFFECT MOVIES

I worked with strobe-effect movies for a few years in the 1990s. Exhibiting them a few times to a very strong response. Here is a partial listing of those movies:

Village 1-8

City 1,2,3

Lands 1,2,3

Sky View

The Untergang Folio

Disparactions

In exhibiting them, what became immediately apparent was the extreme importance of scale: the images were most effective when they were placed at eye level and printed at a size large enough to fill a the field of view for an audience member standing approximately 3-4 feet from the screen with the strobe light pulsating at between 25 and 30 fps and placed directly overhead.

note: all strobes and flickers can cause epileptic seizures in some people and so should be used with caution.

WOUND CULTURE

A spectacle of violence forms around the scene of the crime. The phantom public audience is self-conscious when they encounter the site of violence. It is the "as if" quality of murder sites seen in mass media that create a gathering point around the "wound." The cohesion of civil society is menaced by violence; this is its source of fascination—the threat it poses through its relationship to chaos.

We have become confused about the difference between the monster and the human. Our culture has glamorized the sociopath, elevating the serial killer to a celebrity in cinema. Violence becomes "attractive" through these glamorized images, making the scene of the crime vanish into the environment. This is the culture of wounds.

The horror we should feel when encountering these scenes is strangely absent in the same way the crime scene itself vanishes. Our interest in these scenes is pathological, our blindness neurotic: we do not see because we are accustomed to the horror and have not learned to understand what this horror means. So collectively we reject it, perversely, by expecting it, and demanding ever greater realism in its portrayal. The murderous gaze infests our desire to see the unseen and think the unthinkable. We escape horror by living in a state of elevated, eternal horror. We become inured. Our corruption is complete; we transcend the horror by searching it out. This transcendence is a trap.

In escaping the horror, it surrounds us more intensely then if we had fled it directly. Like all experiences, at its heart, it is a paradox. Violence, like sex, is a taboo for precisely this reason.

SCRIPTS FOR *YEAR*

Original notes on the visual language of Year:

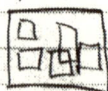 Boxes

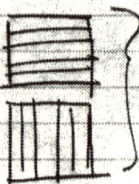 Bars

 Repetition (varying scales)

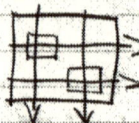 frames

 Divisions

YEAR

OPAQUE

TRANSLUCENT

TRANSPARENT

digital vs analog

- variable speeds
- temporal displacements

Organic

geometric

Many sections use these possibilities in combination, often embedding temporal dislocations (in the form of temporal lenses) in nearly e130very section of Year.

130

Original script for Year

This diagram describes the structural development, color and spatial changes to be employed, and narrative development of the whole.

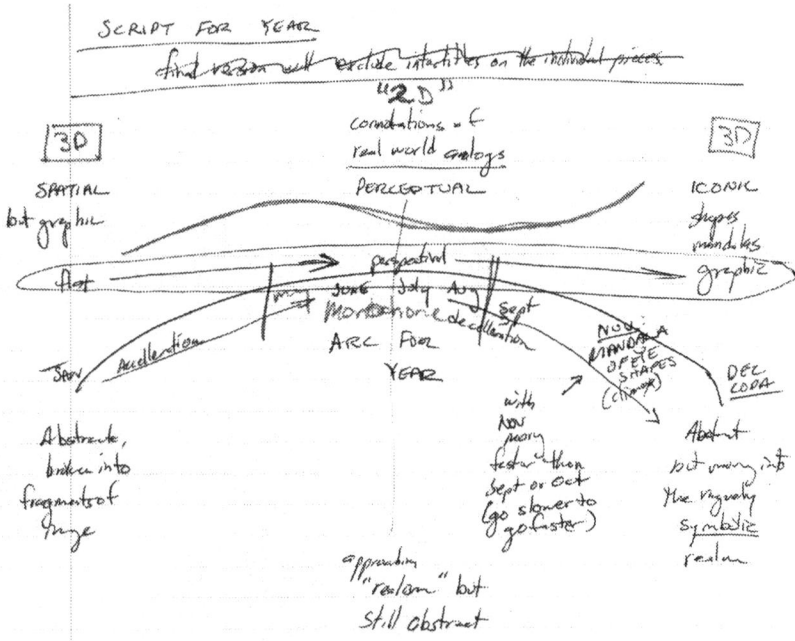

Year was structured to follow a traditional narrative pattern building towards a climax at (nearly) the end.

The creation of a climax had to be built-in from the beginning to make the pacing work over the 20 minute duration of this movie. Structures that develop towards climax must be planned, or else the amount of work reorganizing the whole to present a climax would require changes to the entire structure.

Results from Experimental TV Center Residency **in 2003**

Year was in part the result of a project to work with and in the process compare the new potentials of DV with the older and already realized potentials of analog video. The Experimental Television Center in Owego, NY provided the opportunity to do this research as part of a residency there in 2003.

The conclusion I reached was that DV can do almost everything that analog video can, but with a few exceptions:

ETC - specific materials

1. PAIK-KOBE RASTER
   w/ electromagnetic pulsations,
   distortions to image.

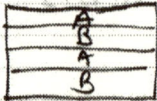

2. images mixed via bars — at level
   of scan lines

3. Oscillator pulses
   as colored marks
   on the video screen

(?) 4. Jones colorizer patterns
   being determined by the
   audio input
   (audio → video)

things that cannot be done (easily/at all)
with digital video

conclusion to residency: that DV is generally
better than analog processing, but
there are a limited number of things DV
can't do (but should) — #1 being the
ability to manipulate individual video fields

On the editing of Year

The interlacing (flicker, pulses, etc.) that appears as occasional "shot" transitions are imitations of the decompression artifacts that can appear in some poorly compressed .mpeg files. Their use in my movies serves a dual role: as a link to the history of film and as a revelation of the artifice of video for those audience members who recognize what these effects "mean" when watching compressed DV.

The insertion of these forms through the editing recreates a glitch that fragments the edit, but elides the actual "cut" as such: instead of cutting, a transition of pulsing flash frames creates a transition from one shot to another, removing the straight cut as such.

Effectively this is an edit that hides the editing in plain sight.

STAN BRAKHAGE
VISIONARY TITLE GENERATOR

How to Use this Title Matrix

Match one word with another on a different line. Any combination of terms is acceptable, as are single-word titles, so long as none of the pairs listed together on the same line are used.

Paranoia . . . . . Corridor

Polite . . . . Madness

Blue . . . . Valve

Shockingly . . . . Hot

Beautiful . . . . . Funerals

Spring . . . . Cycle

Sexual . . . . Saga

Earthen . . . . Aerie

Chartres . . . . Series

Black . . . . Ice

Ephemeral . . . . . Solidity

Three . . . . Homerics

Rage . . . . Net

Christ . . . . Mass

Sex . . . . Dance

Fire . . . . Tree

Crack . . . . Glass

Stellar . . . . Eulogy

City . . . . . . Streaming

Egyptian . . . . Other

Tortured . . . . Dust

Made . . . . Manifest

Star . . . . Garden

Sexual . . . . . Meditation

Zone . . . . Moment

Wonder . . . . Ring

This title generator was used to create titles for some of the New Movies (2001) and New Movies (2002) modular works. It is derived from the collection of Stan Brakhage's movies listed in Canyon Cinema Film/Video Catalog #8 (2000), drawing primarily on 2 word titles. These titles present two terms framed in opposition, and generally have a religious/mythological connotation.

Similar title matrixes could be generated from any set of words. The utility of this matrix is that it allows the creation of suggestive, visionary (even auteurist) titles without the need for subjective "soul searching" to achieve the desired effect: the appearance of subjectivity without necessarily using a subjectivist aesthetic as such (although personal preference does play a role in choosing pairs from this matrix).

Some title possibilities

Paranoia Cycle   Black Eulogy

Egyptian Ice   Wonder Funerals

Tortured Corridor*   Ephemeral Valve

Fire Garden   Spring Ring

Other possible combinations

_____ of _____
      verb   noun
                        adj.

Forces of Symmetry*   Run of Dogs

Breath of Waiting   Rage of Ice

All are suggestive in their own ways . . .

* Indicates titles I used in my movies.

Michael Betancourt can be
reached via the Internet at
michael @ cinegraphic.net

www.cinegraphic.net
 the avant-garde film & video blog

Published by the Wildside Press

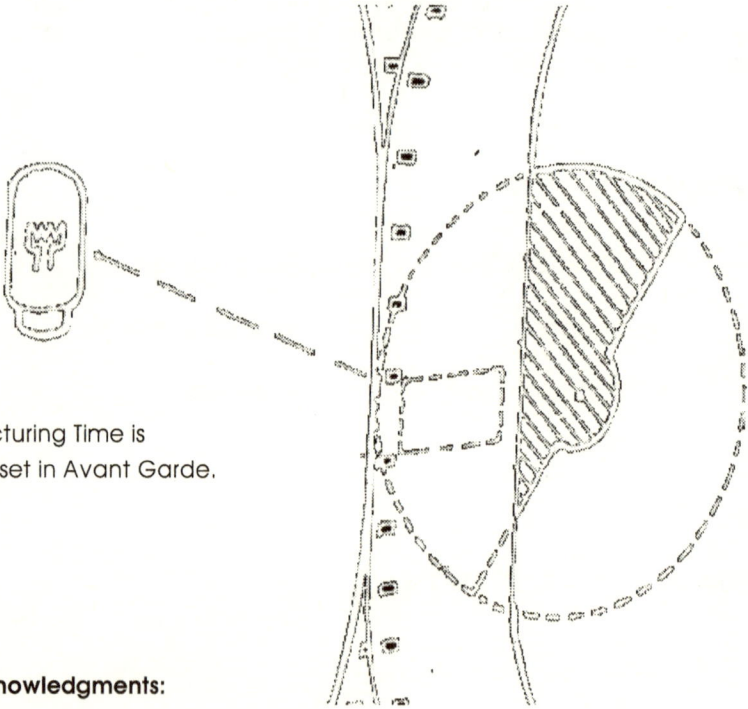

Structuring Time is
typeset in Avant Garde.

Acknowledgments:

Without the following people's
generous support, suggestions and
assistance in the preparation of this
book over the years of revisions,
rewriting, rethinking, and not least
for siting through my experiments:

      Charles Recher,

      Timothy Inners,

      Jacek Kolasinski,

      Leah Gliniewicz,

      and my family

          Thank you.

www.ingramcontent.com/pod-product-compliance
Lightning Source LLC
LaVergne TN
LVHW011334080426
835513LV00006B/335